607 SQUADRON

A SHADE OF BLUE

607 SQUADRON

A SHADE OF BLUE

Robert Dixon

The History Press

This book is dedicated to all who served in 607 (County of Durham) Squadron Auxiliary Air Force

First published 2008

The History Press Ltd
The Mill, Brimscombe Port
Stroud, Gloucestershire, GL5 2QG
www.thehistorypress.co.uk

British Library Cataloguing in Publication Data.
A catalogue record for this book is available from the British Library.

ISBN 978 0 7524 4531 1

Typesetting and origination by The History Press Ltd.
Printed in Great Britain

CONTENTS

LIST OF ABBREVIATIONS

Flt Lt	Flight Lieutenant
F/O	Flying Officer
P/O	Pilot Officer
Sgt	Sergeant
Sqdn Ldr	Squadron Leader

ACKNOWLEDGEMENTS

A book such as this requires a great deal of help as well as encouragement. This has come from a number of sources ranging from organisations down to individuals. Some of these have really bent over backwards in their efforts to provide help. Nicholas Craig has always been a great source of help, allowing me to pillage his father's documents and photo albums, all of which proved invaluable in the research of 607 Squadron; his efforts have gone beyond providing merely help. Likewise, Charles J. Sample was extremely helpful in placing his uncle's photo collection at my disposal. The late William Whitty, one of the 'originals', was always a willing mine of information on all things to do with 607 Squadron.

The Blackadder family are also deserving of special mention for the provision of material from the documents and photographs of the late Francis Blackadder. I also acknowledge their hospitality and their ability and willingness to answer my constant questions and requests. Additionally, I would like to acknowledge the help given by the Turner family in allowing access to the documents and photograph collection of the late Group Captain W.H.N. (Willy) Turner. To Mrs Pamela Turner, in particular, I am indebted for her hospitality in providing not only information but memories of an unforgettable day.

Mrs Davina Helps also deserves many thanks for the provision of documents and a photograph, as well as her welcome hospitality. She and her sister, Cicely Herbert, provided much valuable information on their late father, Dr David Anderson Smith, and their uncle, Launcelot Eustace Smith. Among the many more that need mention are: Aysgarth School; Lansing School; Jen Main of Merchiston School, Edinburgh; Jim Corbett; Maurice Cottam; Bill Norman; Sir Ralph Carr-Ellison KCVO; Paul MacMillan; and Lance Robson, all deserve my thanks. Behind these people are many more individuals – they know who they are and all are deserving of my grateful thanks.

As well as individuals there are a number of organisations, and among these are the 607 Squadron Association, in particular Syd Ashurst and David English. Both have given valuable input and information as well as acting as a sounding board on many occasions. The CWGC also provided much information as always, as did the RAF Historical Branch. The Bundearchiv in both Berlin and Achen provided a great deal of welcome information on the Luftwaffe. The Northumberland Records Office, formerly at Melton Park, Gosforth, also provided a wealth of information, as did the Durham Records Centre.

Various libraries up and down the country provided information and these, too numerous to mention individually, range from the Guild Hall in London, to the City Library in Newcastle upon Tyne and the Northumberland County Library Service. Also worthy of mention are the various newspapers up and down the country, in particular the *Newcastle Journal*, the *Sunderland Echo* and the *Northern Echo*. Various cemeteries and crematoria, ever at the forgotten end when thanks are given, are also deserving of praise. No matter how small the contribution, I thank you all.

Thanks are also due to the publishers, The History Press, for bringing the book to fruition and in particular Amy Rigg for her valuable help and her little extra push at the onset. I would also like to thank my wife, Shirley, for her support and the endless supply of nutrition over a very long period.

INTRODUCTION

It was while researching the Battle of Britain, as it affected the north-east of England, that I first became aware that a number of the pilots who had taken part in this event actually originated from the area. There they were, in the newspapers of the day, and to a lesser extent in books that dealt with the period, although they were often only included in lists. By now, many of these men were virtually forgotten. A little more digging revealed that not only did pilots originate from this area, but a whole squadron as well. This was none other than 607 (County of Durham) Squadron Auxiliary Air Force, to give it its full title, a bomber squadron originally and later a fighter squadron. With the kind help of Nicholas Craig and Charles Sample, a son and nephew respectively, of two former pilots of 607 Squadron, I was given an insight into the squadron by way of collections of photographs. This gave me a unique, pictorial glimpse into the past life of a squadron and a way of life now gone.

The more I looked into these photographs, the more that came to light – it was a squadron's life in pictorial form. Most, if not all, of these photographs have never been aired in public before, coming as they do from private sources. Here were most, possibly all, of the men who had made up that squadron. Here was their life, how they worked and how they played. For some, their time was to be all too short and their life ended even before the war began. Others were destined not to last the war; their lives cut short by that conflict. More than a few were destined to have their flying career cut short during the war years but managed to fight a different war; a war from behind the barbed wire of a PoW camp. For a select few, the war years were only an extension of their flying career, and their career was to be a long and sometimes distinguished one.

So, what was known of this squadron? The answer was quite simple: very little. They are, of course, given general mention in books that deal with the various theatres of the war that the squadron took part in. Books on the Auxiliary Air Force (AAF) do exist and 607 Squadron is given a more in-depth view within those. However, these are generalisations of the squadron at best; there was something missing. What of the squadron's very lifeblood, its pilots? Of course, some are given a mention in the volumes that specialise in pilots as a subject; however, most appear to be tainted and littered with mistakes. What of that great fount of learning and knowledge, the internet? Well, it only brings up what has been put in and not many have put anything in, at least as far as 607 Squadron are concerned. The local press occasionally mentions 607 Squadron, usually in sensationalist form. The squadron's former home base of Usworth, now an aviation museum, does not overburden its visitors with the history of 607 Squadron. What of those pilots who had gone before, the pilots who had helped form this squadron? Of these pilots there is today little trace. Some never even reached the war period, and therefore history, biased towards the war years only, has passed them by and cast them aside as if they never existed in the first place.

This is not a squadron history as such; I leave that to someone more suitably qualified. It is an appreciation of a bomber squadron, and later a fighter squadron, as seen through the eyes of its own pilots. It forms a picture of a squadron in both peace and war, as seen by a group of men acknowledged as being 'better off' than the average, but also a band of young men bonded together by their shared sense of territory, which is somewhat different from the more generally held 'men from every walk of life' view. This statement was simply not true – all of the men who formed the nucleus of 607 Squadron originated from backgrounds that afforded them time away from their employment. They were part of a certain class which allowed them the privilege to be flexible in their work time.

My own research, covered in this book, comes to an end, as far as 607 Squadron goes, in early 1941. This is not without reason. My interest is mainly in the men of an Auxiliary Air Force Squadron and, therefore, their territorial life as it interacted with that squadron. With the beginning of the Second World War, the AAF was embodied into the Royal Air Force (RAF). One became part of the other. Although the squadron was to retain its territorial connections after this, it was slowly to diminish, as first the Battle of France followed by the Battle of Britain took their toll on the squadron's pilots. Regular RAF personnel replaced the fallen and the pilots who were posted on to other units. 607 Squadron lost its original Auxiliary feel and individuality as it became another squadron of the RAF.

CHAPTER ONE

THE BEGINNINGS

With the onset of the Second World War, many of the Auxiliary Air Force squadrons were among the first to taste the real action against the enemy. Indeed, as the war progressed, there were many 'firsts' created among the ranks of the AAF. The first enemy aircraft brought down on the British mainland in the conflict was brought down by an AAF squadron; in fact there were two squadrons: 602 and 603. A Heinkel He III was destroyed in the Lammermuir Hills to the south of Edinburgh. The same squadrons were responsible for bringing down the first enemy aircraft of the war: a Junkers Ju 88 that fell into the sea off Port Seton near Edinburgh. As the war moved on, operations frequently demanded specialised techniques such as pinpoint bombing. Another 'first' was gained by 607 Squadron in 1941 when it became the first squadron to operate the 'Hurri' bomber, the Hawker Hurricane with bombs attached. Yet another Auxiliary Air Force squadron came to the fore: 613 Squadron, with its Mosquito fighter-bombers successfully attacking the Gestapo headquarters in The Hague.

Today, these squadrons are thought of as an extension of the RAF squadrons. However, there was a difference. In their beginnings these squadrons, numbering twenty-one, were until after the outbreak of war manned by part-timers. Apart from flying these men also held down other, regular employment. These men, like the squadrons they flew with, were thought of as just an extension of the RAF. Many of these part-timers were to bear the brunt of the air fighting in the battles over France as well as the Battle of Britain. In today's modern world of 'plastic heroes' most of these men are put to one side and, in many cases, forgotten altogether. Who among the modern society can forget the heroism of 'The Great Escape'? Some, if asked, could tell you that it was led by a certain Sqdn Ldr, Roger Bushell. What is not so well known is that Sqdn Ldr Bushell was an AAF officer, a part-timer.

The First World War had brought about many changes, one of which was trench warfare. Horses were still in use, yet alongside them came the tank. The Royal Navy saw the last days of its large battle fleets standing square on to that of the enemy as they attempted to batter each other into submission. Into the war drifted a new type of war machine: the flying machine, the aeroplane. Primarily, the aeroplane was in use as a reconnaissance machine, used to gather information for the Army as well as 'spot' for the artillery. These flimsy 'playthings' were considered as not to be taken too seriously, and the men who flew them were deemed expendable. Things were to change, however, when it was found that bombs could be carried on aeroplanes. They could now destroy targets much further behind the enemy lines, and act as an extension of the artillery.

Things were to change once more when someone found a way of attaching guns to these same aeroplanes. Now they could shoot down enemy aircraft that were carrying bombs. As each air force built up their air arm, their fighters, first known as scouts, could now fight each other. A new breed of men was born in this air fighting: the fighter pilot. The air force was now a true all-round fighting machine. As hostilities came to an end in 1918 the government of the day had to cut back on spending. The first cuts invariably occured in the same place: the defences of the country. Many of the squadrons of the newly formed RAF were now disbanded.[1] However, many had other ideas. An Air Force Constitution of 1917 called for the provision of an Air Force Reserve as well as an Auxiliary Air Force. The new arm of the Air Force was to be formed on a part-time basis and, in a memorandum of 1919, Sir Hugh Trenchard called for the reserve air force to be formed on a territorial basis. Men would be drawn from their own areas. They would train part-time in their own area. That they all lived in the same area would help give them a sense of purpose. A Bill was not drawn up until 1922 and, when presented, fell short of the backing needed to see it through. The result was that the Bill did not become law until 1924.

The then Secretary of State for Air, Sir Samuel Hoare, stated:

> Trenchard envisaged the Auxiliary as a corps d'elite comprised of the kind of young men who earlier would have been interested in horses, but who now wished to serve their country in machines. He conceived the new mechanical yeomanry with its aeroplanes based on the great centres of industry.

Esprit de corps was to be the dominating force in the squadrons and each, therefore, was to have a well-equipped headquarters, mess, and distinctive life of its own. Social meetings were to be encouraged and on no account was any squadron to be regarded as a reserve for filling up regular units. The forebodings of the doubters and critics were soon proved groundless. So, far from non-regular units damaging the reputations of the regular squadrons, they actually added some of the most glorious pages to the history of the RAF during the Second World War.

This had been the dream of Trenchard from the start. The AAF squadrons were to be seen as part of the RAF, whether bomber or fighter squadrons; they were not to be looked upon as a stopgap or filler while other, regular squadrons were performing other duties. The esprit de corps was to be a fundamental principle in the Auxiliary squadrons. In fact; it was almost to be the backbone of the AAF. It is important to remember that these squadrons were recruited on a local basis. Most of the men in the squadrons, ground crew as well as aircrew, would have a shared identity. They may not have exactly known each and every other person on the squadron but they would be aware of their background. A strong sense of community spirit would survive among the Auxiliary squadrons. In one way this could be seen as a good thing – a shared past that would see these men through any hardship. However, the conflict that lay in the future would test that community spirit. No one knew how the loss of a comrade would affect a squadron that had been formed from one area. The squadron, apart from being a military fighting unit, was almost a family.

The original plan for the AAF was that six squadrons should be formed, with a further seven making up the special reserve. The squadrons of the latter were to be made up of four squadrons with single-engine bombers, and a further four squadrons equipped with twin-engine bombers. Long-term plans were for twenty squadrons in all to form the AAF; the squadrons to be placed strategically around the country. These squadrons, as visualized by Trenchard, were to be raised and maintained within their own areas. In times of conflict, these squadrons would become part of the air defence of Great Britain. The squadrons were to be based at a regular aerodrome within the vicinity of the town from which the recruits were drawn. This aerodrome, in any national emergency, would act as the squadron's war station. The personnel would be kept at their training optimum by attending the aerodrome on a regular basis, normally about two nights a week.

Of course, the squadrons of the AAF had to have commanding officers and these men would have to be pre-trained. Therefore they would have to come from within the RAF. A small nucleus of trained and regular RAF personnel would also have to be posted in to the squadrons in order to carry out the training. At a later date the rules were changed slightly, allowing the commanding officer to be a non-regular officer, although his staff had to be regular officers in order to carry out the flying training. The recruits themselves had to be a minimum of eighteen years of age, with an upper limit set at no more than twenty-five unless the new recruit had already served a term as a regular officer. In that case the upper age limit was raised to thirty-one. Of course, one attraction was to stand out against any other. Those who joined, as would-be pilots, would learn to fly at the expense of the government.

As well as taking up this training schedule, the fact still remained that fledgling pilots still had to have secure jobs outside the flying training regime. This employment not only had to pay them well enough, it had also to be flexible enough to allow time off for training purposes. It can, therefore, be seen that most of these men would come from a certain section of society. They had to be well off, and many would look upon AAF pilots as being of the 'country bumpkin' type or from the hunting and shooting fraternity. Certainly, Johnnie Johnson's experience demonstrates this. When it was learned, during an interview to join the AAF, that Johnnie Johnson came from Leicestershire, he was asked which pack he followed. When it was learned that Johnnie spent all his spare cash on flying lessons (the main reason he was facing the interview), the interview was hastily terminated.[2] Johnnie Johnson was later, after a short period in the Territorial Army, to join the RAFVR, and the rest is history.

Sir Samuel Hoare had stated, as seen already, that the AAF had been '... successful from the beginning'. However, this was not strictly true. Already living two very different lives – the life of the working civilian and the service pilot – the pilots of the Auxiliary Air Force were looked upon with wonder in both aspects of their lives. As a third dimension, their more professional comrades of the RAF looked down on them with a jaundiced eye. In 1937 a young Peter Townsend, back from service in the Far East and serving at Tangmere at the time, found that the RAF was populated by new faces due to the rise

Squadron Leader
Leslie Runciman.

Leslie Ranchman's private aircraft at Leyland.

W.H.N. (Willy) Turner. (Family of Group Captain W.H.N. Turner)

of German power; the RAF had expanded. What was thought of as the 'best little flying club in the world' had gone and in its place was a 'force', a national air arm. The RAF was now populated with, '… strange faces, different people with a different style'. Townsend resented these men who, he thought, had '… answered the RAF's urgent appeal and found heaven-sent relief from boring civilian jobs'. At that time Townsend was to look on these men as, 'parvenu pilots'.[3] Later, during the war years, Townsend was to have a change of heart towards these men, as they made up most of the squadrons that he was to fly with as well as command.

The comments of Peter Townsend do not appear to be an isolated case. With the Battle of Britain well and truly engaged, 603 (City of Edinburgh) Squadron flew into Hornchurch on 23 August. The pilots climbed from their Spitfires and made their way across the airfield. The manner of their commanding officer was observed as:

> … getting out of his Spitfire with his forage-cap perched on the back of his head and mean-dering towards the control tower with bent shoulders, hands in pockets, followed by the motliest collection of unmilitary-looking young men that he'd seen for a very long time. He was amazed, and then remembered that No.603 was an Auxiliary squadron. That explained it, but 'Why', he thought, 'should they be unloaded on him?'[4]

So thought Group Captain C.A. Bouchier, Station Commander of RAF Hornchurch. It is clear that a sense of prejudice against these part-timers existed well after the advent of war and was to last well into the conflict, if not to the end of it.

The press of the day also looked on the members of the Auxiliary Air Force as a bit of a joke. To the press they were the 'long-haired boys', the 'weekend flyers' or the 'part-timers'. Of course, there was some basis for these views, even if they were blinkered. Regular RAF personnel had to endure much ground training before they got their hands anywhere near an aeroplane. They also had to face training to become an officer and a gentleman. Just prior to the war years, when the RAFVR came into being, their person-nel, even when they had qualified as pilots, were mostly to retain the rank of Sergeant. The personnel of the Auxiliary Air Force had little of this training, and even that was part-time. Whatever drills they had were usually held in conjunction with the Territorial Army. The flying training was equally leisurely and, after only a few flights, the Auxiliary pilot attained officer rank. Therefore, all flying members of an Auxiliary squadron were of officer rank from the very start; there were no non-commissioned flying personnel. However, promotion was limited. Prior to the outbreak of war, there were few pilots of Flight Lieutenant rank, as this was the rank of the Flight Commanders and there were only two Flight Commanders on each squadron.

However, as the press made its derogatory remarks about the RAF, and the AAF in particular, it could be seen that this same press gave a shop window to aviation and, ulti-mately, the success of both the RAF and the AAF. Whilst the First World War years had seen the development of the aeroplane as a military machine, the majority of the public knew little of such things. Knowledge of the aeroplane was mainly gleaned from grainy photographs in the newspapers of the day, as well as equally grainy and jerky moving footage at the local cinema. To see an aeroplane fly over your house was not an everyday occurrence, and airfields, particularly the further north you travelled, were equally sparse. It was during this period, however, that certain names began to appear in the press and on film. Names such as Captain John Alcock and Lieutenant Arthur Whitten Brown suddenly sprang to the fore. They had become the first to fly non-stop across the Atlantic, making the crossing in less than 16½ hours on 14–15 June 1919. Of course, both men were knighted for their pioneering achievement. The same pioneering achievement was to make the newspaper headlines with: 'Alcock and Brown fly across the Atlantic; Make 1,980 miles in 16 hours, 12 minutes; Sometimes upside down in dense, icy fog.' Daring headlines such as this in the *New York Times* would catch the eye and thrust aviation to the fore.

Charles Lindberg was to add to the legend when he became the first to fly the Atlantic single handed in 1927. Not to be outdone by the so far male-dominated pursuit of flying, Amelia Earhart became the first female pilot to fly solo across that great divide, on 17–18 June 1928. Thereafter, setting up records kept aviation in the eye of the press and its public. In May 1930, British female pilot Amy Johnson, a former typist from Hull, broke the world solo record flying from Croydon, England, to Australia. Her flight, from an England still emerging from the after-effects of a world war as well as the Depression, made Amy Johnson a star on a world stage. Once more, aviation was thrust onto the billboards of the world press with headlines such as: 'She's there' and 'Amy's Triumph'. Even a song was written about the British aviatrix, titled simply: 'Wonderful Amy.' The British press had been captured by the growing interest in aviation.

As the 1930s advanced, so did the world of aviation. Distance flights, solo and accompanied, altitude records, speed records and air races all kept aviation in the eye of the public. Amy Johnson flew solo from Croydon to Cape Town in a Puss Moth named *Desert Cloud* in November of 1932. The previous year she had terminated her flight from England to Tokyo, Japan. In 1933, together with her new husband Jim Mollison, Amy flew the Atlantic from east to west, making a forced landing in Bridgetown, Connecticut. In 1934, what was termed as 'The Great 1934 London–Melbourne Race' was underway, sponsored by Australian confectionary giant Sir MacPherson Robertson (known as 'MacRobertson'). It was this race that saw the emergence of the custom-built de Havilland DH 88 Comet, three of which were entered in the race in an attempt to bring aviation glory to Britain. Lloyds of London gave the odds of being killed in such a race as 1 in 12. C.W.A. Scott and T. Campbell Black won the race in their red-painted Comet named *Grosvenor House*. The Mollisons' Comet, *Black Magic*, was forced out of the race with engine trouble. It was, of course, aviation feats such as these that thrust aeroplanes and their pilots into the headlines of the press and onto a world stage, the point being to keep aviation in the minds of not only would-be pilots, but also a public looking beyond the effects of a world war. However, little known at that time, new events were taking place in central Europe – the Nuremberg Rallies were getting underway.

The press, however, was not the only source to bring aviation to the general public. In the 1920s Alan Cobham began to tour Britain in a war surplus Avro 504. It was in this that he gave many a paying passenger their first taste of flight. As an ex-war pilot, knighted in 1926, he formed the National Aviation Day (later Display) Company Ltd, later to become known as Sir Alan Cobham's Flying Circus. This touring aviation com-

An early flight for W.H.N. (Willy) Turner, centre. (Family of Group Captain W.H.N. Turner)

pany specialised in stunt flying, flying displays, wing walking and parachuting. Travelling to most of the country, it brought aviation to the masses and did much to popularise flying. The cheap ride also gained popularity. Other, smaller touring aviation ventures were also spawned around this time, each one cashing in. It was these touring businesses where many future pilots gained their first air experience. A photograph of 1920s vintage does exist of one such venture. An aeroplane of The Cornwall Aviation Company Ltd has a young boy in one of its seats – W.H.N. Turner – who years later was to become a flying instructor on 607 Squadron. It is known that, during 1930, Sir Alan Cobham's Flying Circus did pay a visit to Usworth. Although the crowd were thrilled by the event, seeing these strange aircraft in the skies over Sunderland at first hand, it is not known how many of the future pilots from Sunderland actually witnessed the event.

The 1930s came as a new dawn for the RAF and the fledgling AAF. The country was still suffering the after-effects of the First World War, as well as hardship among its people. The RAF came into being on 1 April 1918, and had been developed up to a certain point as the Royal Flying Corps (RFC). By the end of the First World War it had served its purpose and its equipment was allowed to deteriorate. This deterioration meant that by 1929 the aircraft used were little different from those that had fought during the war. As for the RAF, it had been kept at a level where it came to be known as the best flying club in the world. However, with the 1930s the RAF, and with it the emerging AAF, entered what was to become known as the 'Golden Age of Flying'. Aircraft, although technologically not much different from those of the war years, became more prominent with the emerging air displays that forced them into the eye of the public. Gone was the drab camouflage, and in its place came bright colours and natural finishes, the aircraft giving flying displays of tight precision never seen before. It was in the wake of this euphoria that the AAF came into being, and soon they would be sharing the skies as they put on their own flying displays on the Empire Flying Days that began a few years later.

There were, however, differences between Auxiliary Air Force members and those of the RAF. One great advantage the Auxiliary airman had over his RAF counterpart was their condition of service. Once an Auxiliary airman, officer or NCO had signed on with the AAF, he could not be posted on to another squadron without his consent. This had the advantage of giving the squadron and its members a feeling of stability, territorialism and security, and this is what Trenchard had set out to do. All members of an Auxiliary squadron shared this same territorialism, this same sense of background. However, it stopped short of sharing the class system. As with the RAF, the AAF officers and other ranks were always apart.

It was, of course, the cultural background that on one hand held them together, while on the other it separated them. They may have shared the same territorial background but personal background was always going to be different. The officer candidate, unlike his RAF counterpart was alway,s of necessity, a man of near-independent means. In most cases they came from a family background that, more often then not, owned the business they worked in. They could afford to take time off during the week to do their training. They could also take time off to attend the summer camps for training. For the other ranks, however, things were not so straightforward. The men of the other ranks could ill afford to take time off work, and usually this amounted to a great deal of personal hardship. Certainly the summer camp for the other ranks meant only one thing – gone was the family holiday. They were only allowed two weeks away from work and that was taken up with the training. For two weeks the airmen would live the life of their RAF counterparts. The upside of this being that they were paid the same as the regular airmen.

Entrance into the AAF was not too easy, even for the officer candidate. Firstly, entrance was severely limited. Once in, an officer rarely left. When he did, the vacancy had many applicants, with the limitation being that an application was by recommendation only. Therefore, an officer candidate had to know someone who was already a serving officer. The application was followed by an interview with the squadron adjutant, a regular RAF officer and therefore not always a man from the candidate's own social standing. An air experience flight was then arranged, again with the squadron adjutant who was also the squadron flying instructor. If this went well the aspiring candidate was then passed on to the commanding officer, the interview normally taking the form of a house visit, bringing the Commander's wife into the equation. If this went well, then the candidate was usually accepted.

That there was always a difference between the regular RAF officers and those of the AAF has already been shown in the statements of Peter Townsend and Group Captain C.A. Bouchier. However, the differing views were not all one-sided. The AAF could be seen to be encouraging this difference of opinion. Certainly, H.S.L. Dundas, who was to begin his service life with 616 (South Yorkshire) Squadron, saw the AAF as something apart from the RAF, if not above it. He shared the outlook of Trenchard that the AAF could and should be seen as the 'Royal Yacht Squadron' of the RAF and at the head of the RAF. Hugh Dundas also saw the AAF as assuming '… a character closely resembling that of the crack cavalry units of earlier times'. For Hugh Dundas, therefore, the AAF was an elitist unit, a leader rather than a follower. In a bid to further themselves from the regular RAF, an AAF officer could, and often did, personalise his uniform. Gone was the standard, dark-grey lining of the RAF uniform tunic and greatcoat, and in its place was a scarlet red one. Also recorded by Hugh Dundas was the fact that the AAF officer would often frequent Gieves of Saville Row, London, not only to have their clothes made but even their helmets. The country gentleman, which many AAF Officers were, always had to be seen as properly dressed, even if their outfit was a government uniform.

With Trenchard's dream now a reality we can take a more in-depth look at a squadron. In this case it is to be 607 (County of Durham) Squadron, the most northerly of the English squadrons. Two further squadrons were based in Scotland: 602 (City of Glasgow) and 603 (City of Edinburgh). What kind of men were these part-time flyers? 607 Squadron was average in the Auxiliary Air Force, although its members probably regarded it as the best. For our purpose, it was an illustration of Auxiliary life.

Notes

1. Tony Ross (ed.), *75 Eventful Years' Tribute to the Royal Air Force*, p.9, was to note that the RAF was reduced from its wartime strength of around 280 squadrons to a number one tenth that size.
2. Johnnie Johnson in *Wing Leader*, p.17.
3. Peter Townsend, *Time and Chance*, p.95.
4. Bruce Robertson, *Spitfire – The Story of a Famous Fighter*, pp.38–9.

CHAPTER TWO

A SQUADRON IS BORN

607 Squadron, the newest of the Auxiliary Air Force Squadrons, came into being during the spring of 1930. It was officially and grandly named 607 (County of Durham) (Bomber) Squadron, Auxiliary Air Force. The site picked to house the airfield of this new squadron was a former First World War aerodrome known as North Hylton. North Hylton, as its name implies, lies in the Hylton area about 1 mile to the west of the industrial town of Sunderland. It was 36 Squadron who had last used this airfield during the First World War, flying their BE 2Cs and BE 12s, later replaced by FE 2Bs. When 36 Squadron departed North Hylton in 1919, it was left to fall into disuse and so it remained until reactivated for 607 Squadron. The honour of being the first officer to arrive on the squadron fell to Flt Lt M. Wiblin. Flt Lt Wiblin, a regular officer in the RAF, was posted onto the squadron on 17 March 1930. Flt Lt Wiblin was the squadron adjutant and flying instructor, although the squadron had no aircraft but no personnel. Next man to arrive on the embryonic squadron was F/O M. Griffiths, arriving on 6 May to take up his post as assistant adjutant and flying instructor to Flt Lt Wiblin. It was not until 13 June that the new commanding officer was to arrive. Sqdn Ldr Walter Leslie Runciman was gazetted to a commission in the Auxiliary Air Force and appointed to 607 Squadron as its commanding officer. Sqdn Ldr Runciman was the first of the part-timers to join the squadron. His full-time employment was being part of the family shipping business known as the Moor Line, based in Newcastle upon Tyne. It was these three men who would be responsible for the forming of 607 Squadron.

The birth of the squadron was to prove to be a leisurely affair. It had three officers but no aircraft and no real airfield to speak of. The airfield was still in the planning stages and was not laid out until October 1931. At this stage it was still only a wooden-hutted camp and it would take another year before it was developed enough to call itself an air-field. From then on, it would come to be known under its new name, Usworth, a name taken from a nearby village. Although still without aircraft, some of the staff were already being replaced. F/O G O St G. Morris replaced F/O M. Griffiths as adjutant and flying instructor from 5 January 1932, with F/O L.H. Anness AFC appointed to the squadron as stores officer on the same date. Later in the year, on 21 September, Dr David Anderson Smith of Newcastle upon Tyne was appointed as medical practitioner to the squadron. Dr Smith was a Scot by birth, eventually settling in Newcastle upon Tyne. His neighbour at the time was Leslie Runciman, who had a town house there. It is thought that this was the connection which eventually brought Dr Smith into contact with 607 Squadron. The advance party, the nucleus of 607 Squadron, arrived at Usworth on 30 September and was a little dismayed. The adjutant, his assistant, as well as the stores officer and some twelve NCOs, were faced with an airfield that was only partly completed. There was a distinct lack of footpaths and connecting, serviceable roads. All this would create problems with the delivery and distribution of stores and equipment.

Apart from the minor teething problems, the squadron was still without its main ingredient: aircraft. The first aircraft to land at Usworth as a squadron aircraft was a Gypsy Moth flown in from Hendon, arriving on 25 October 1932. This aircraft was parked in the squadron's first hangar, a Herview hangar that became the bane of the squadron maintenance crews, as it was in constant need of attention due to damage by the winds. A Lamella hangar eventually replaced the first in 1933. The new squadron consisted of forty-four men in all and most of those were put to work moving around the squadron equipment and carrying out the general fatigue work. A notable day for the squadron was 3 December 1932. On this day, the squadron's first Westland Wapiti aircraft arrived,

Dr David Anderson Smith, squadron doctor. (Mrs Davina Helps)

A silver cigarette box – a wedding present from 607 Squadron to Dr D.A. Smith. (Author)

the two-seat light bomber that would form the squadron's complement of aircraft. The Wapiti was flown in from Hendon, followed shortly afterwards by two Avro 504s; one flown in from RAF Manston and the other from RAF Thornaby. The aircraft, brought in for training, were soon put to good use in their role by Leslie Runciman, who took the chance to get in as much flying practice as possible, even though he was a proficient civilian pilot. The aircraft were also used in the *ab initio* training of the first squadron trainee pilots, the first two being Launcelot Eustice Smith, known as Launce, from Hexham, Northumberland, who was part of the Smiths Dock Ship Building and Repair Company; and James Anderson Vick of Newcastle upon Tyne. The training and recruiting of squadron personnel was still being carried out at what seemed to be a leisurely pace. Although many candidates for flying duties had been interviewed, most, for one reason or another, were classed as unsuitable. Likewise, little attempt was made to recruit airmen for the ground trades, the feeling being that it was better to wait until the squadron had a recognisable airfield.

Both Launce Smith and James Vick were to receive their 'A' licence during this year, while the squadron was to receive more aircraft. Four service Westland Wapiti aircraft were flown into Usworth with another Avro 504 bringing the squadron complement to nine. Although still small in number, the squadron's annual AOCs inspection was carried out by Air Commodore W.F. MacNeeve Foster CB, DSO, DFC. F/O E.G. Moore, who had joined the squadron as stores officer in May 1933, was posted to Iraq in February 1934, his place being taken by F/O G.J. Gaynor. Dr David Anderson Smith, a brother-in-law of pilot Launce Smith, was granted a commission as an F/O, Medical Branch, on 2 July 1933. Eventually he was to leave the RAF with the rank of Wing Commander,

Jim Vick in a Westland Wapiti. (607 (County of Durham) Squadron Association)

while Flt Lt M. Wiblin, the squadron's first adjutant and flying instructor, was posted to Aden Command on 2 February 1934. During March and April 1934, a further four Wapiti aircraft were flown into Usworth, bringing the squadron strength of Wapiti aircraft up to nine and the full squadron complement of aircraft to twelve.

Along with the new aircraft came the new pilots. Leslie Runciman and his adjutants picked the squadron pilots with care. Among the new arrivals was Joseph R. Kayll, who worked in the Sunderland timber business of Joseph Thompson. Maurice Milne Irving, known as 'Milne', came from the Jesmond area of Newcastle upon Tyne and worked as an engineer in the locomotive division of Armstrong Whitworth. John Ellis Macomb was a trained solicitor and had worked in the legal department of Lancashire County Council.[1] John McComb was later to transfer to 600 (City of London) (B) Squadron on 17 April 1934. John McComb was to serve throughout the war and left the RAF with the rank of Wing Commander. He died in August 1988. John Sample, a land agent from Longhirst, Northumberland, was to join the squadron on 27 April. Will Gore, an electrical engineer with Reyrolle Research, from Middlesbrough, also joined the squadron during this period, followed by Theodore Ralph Tate Carr-Ellison, son of Herbert George Carr-Ellison, a solicitor from Guyzance, Northumberland. Leslie Runciman had picked his men from a wide range of the area covering a diverse background.

An open day was held on 24 May 1934 under the heading of Empire Air Day. This was not only a squadron first, but a first for the RAF as well. The RAF and, on this

An Avro 504 at Usworth. (Family of John Sample)

Westland Wapiti of 607 Squadron at Sunderland Air Show.

A Westland Wapiti. (607 (County of Durham) Squadron Association)

Westland Wapiti. (Family of John Sample)

occasion, the AAF put themselves on show to the general public. Around 13,000 visitors were to cram into Usworth to look over the aircraft and especially 'their' squadron. Around another 5,000 contented themselves with viewing the air display from outside the airfield perimeter. An Honorary Air Commodore was chosen for the squadron – the man chosen to perform this office was Charles Stewart Henry Vane-Tempest-Stewart, otherwise known as the 7th Marquess of Londonderry. Son of the 6th Marquess of Londonderry, he had houses in London and estates in Northern Ireland, at Mount Stewart and County Durham, at Wynyard Hall near Stockton. Among his local business ventures were the coalmines, mostly in the Seaham area of County Durham. The 7th Marquess of Londonderry began his honorary role with 607 Squadron in 1934. At that time he was well in the limelight, and therefore his story needs to be given a little airing.

The young Vane-Tempest-Stewart was born on 13 May 1878, just around the corner from Buckingham Palace in Eaton Place, London. He was the second child and eldest son of the 6th Marquess of Londonderry and also a cousin of Winston Churchill, a man he was destined to clash with in later years. Education was by way of Eton College followed by a spell in the Royal Military College at Sandhurst. He was commissioned into the Royal Horse Guards under his courtesy title of Viscount Castlereagh. However, the 6th Marquess saw his son's career as being in politics and cajoled him until he finally moved onto that route. He eventually paid back his father's persistence by becoming the Conservative MP for Maidstone in 1906, before vacating the office to return to Army life in the First World War. Back in the Royal Horse Guards, he was mentioned in dispatches twice, and eventually left the Army with the rank of Lieutenant Colonel at the end of hostilities.

Back in politics once more, he became the Under Secretary of State for Air on his second attempt, having been more than a bit 'miffed' at not being accepted on his first attempt. However, he soon became disillusioned and departed to Northern Ireland to take up office there in 1921. In the General Strike of 1926, he fought the corner of the moderate, using his experience as a mine owner to his advantage and winning much support for his stance. He returned once more to take his seat in Stanley Baldwin's cabinet of 1928, and in 1931 he became the Secretary for Air. As a pilot himself, he held out strongly against any disarmament and was an advocate of the bombers' strategy while policing in the far-flung countries. His opposing stance against the cabinet, however, led to him being dubbed a 'warmonger', and he was removed from his Air Ministry post in the spring of 1935.

It was during this period that an expansion programme came into being. Relieved of his Air Ministry post, Londonderry sought to vindicate himself once more, and to this end he began a series of visits to Germany. While there, he was wined and dined by the elite of the Nazi party, and was a guest of Herman Goering and also met Adolf Hitler. Rather than this plan vindicating him, he lost any support from the British, who lost no time in brandishing him as Hitler's friend at worst, and leaning too far to the Germans at best. On Whit Sunday 1936, nine officers and one airman of 607 Squadron made the flight to Newtonards at the request of the Marquess of Londonderry. Members of 602 and 603 Squadrons were already there. Among the other guests, however, was the German Ambassador, Joachim von Ribbentrop, his wife and entourage. The German party flew in the previous Friday in a Junkers Ju 52; the aircraft of 607 Squadron lined up alongside it. A party was held at Londonderry's home, Mount Stewart. Londonderry and his German guests sat at a table in the centre while the pilots sat at small tables set around the periphery. His chief guest, von Ribbentrop, presented Londonderry with a Meissen porcelain figurine, representing a Nazi Stormtrooper. Today, the porcelain figurine still sits on the mantelpiece in Mount Stewart.

Londonderry's apparent leaning towards Nazi Germany did much to damage his political career and it has certainly overshadowed any good that he did. He had fought strongly for modern air defences and had encouraged the early planning of both the Spitfire and the Hurricane, as well as fighting for the development of the use of radar for the RAF. It was during his time as Air Minister that the RAF College at Cranwell came into being. However, despite all this, he is most remembered as being Hitler's friend, or at the very least for leaning too far towards Nazi Germany. He was certainly headstrong and not a team player. In his leanings towards Nazi Germany he was perhaps more than a little naïve.

With the ending of his tenure, after five years Lord Londonderry's association with 607 Squadron came to an end. He was involved in a glider accident in 1945, the after-effects leaving him in a weakened state. A succession of strokes led to his eventual death at his home in Mount Stewart on 11 February 1949. He was buried three days later in the grounds of Mount Stewart.

A highlight in the squadron's calendar was its annual summer camp. These were to be held at various RAF stations throughout Britain, the main idea being to give the squadron intensive training, especially alongside other Auxiliary or regular RAF squadrons. The first annual summer camp was held on 1 September 1934 at RAF Leuchars, Fife, Scotland. The officers flew up to Leuchars in the squadron's aircraft while the airmen travelled by road and rail transport. An inspection was carried out during the camp; this was carried out by the air officer commanding. In 1934 this was Air Commodore J.E.A. Baldwin, DSO, OBE. Inspection was normally followed by a fly-past of the squadron aircraft; however, this was put back to the following morning, 8 September, due to bad weather. On 15 September, the squadron returned south to Usworth with the exception of the aircraft. Once again, bad weather had intervened and the squadron's aircraft returned to Usworth the following day.

The next pilot to join the squadron was Douglas Redington, gazetted on 19 November 1934, who increased the number of officers, including the CO, to thirteen. M.R. Price (F/O RAF ret.) arrived on the squadron to take on the duties of civil stores officer on 31 June. Later he was granted the rank of Flying Officer AAF, as of 7 February 1935. The number of Westland Wapiti aircraft on the squadron strength had increased to twelve, along with the three Avro 504s and one Gypsy Moth. Night flying was introduced to the flying training programme, and by February 1935 at least five pilots had gone solo on night flying. During April, another 'first' was gained by the squadron, a first that they would rather forget. Pilot officer Samuel Sprot, who had joined the squadron on 4 August 1934, became the squadron's first fatality when he was killed in a civil flying accident.[2] No doubt this was to affect the squadron greatly.

Affiliation exercises were carried out with 3 Squadron between 4–5 and 11–12 May. In this Jubilee year for King George V, many celebrations were to be held and among them

607 Squadron's first group photograph at Leuchars in 1934. (607 (County of Durham) Squadron Association)

607 Squadron group photograph at Usworth, 1937. From rear left to right: Dob Wardale, George Wilson, Blackadder, Richardson, Bazin, Redington, Pumphrey, Dixon. Front, left to right: Carr-Ellison, White, Irving, Smith, Manton, Runciman, Quinell, John Bartlett, Vick, Kayll, Sample, Gore. (Family of John Sample)

was a parade in Newcastle upon Tyne. It fell to 607 Squadron to play a part in the fly-past, providing five Wapiti aircraft to fly in formation over the Town Moor with the Lord Mayor of Newcastle taking the salute. Further personnel were to arrive on the squadron during this time, among them George White, who was granted a commission as P/O in the administration department on 29 May, and Thomas Templar Richardson, known as 'Tim', son of Judge Thomas Richardson, OBE, from Corbridge, Northumberland, on 4 June 1935. The following month another first came the way of 607 Squadron. This was King George V's review, to be held at RAF Mildenhall, Suffolk. The review, held on 6 July, had some 356 aircraft on show along with thirty-eight squadrons demonstrating their power in front of King George V, Edward, Prince of Wales, and George, Duke of York. Sqdn Ldr Runciman, Flt Lt N.C. Singer, Jim Vick, Milne Irving, John Sample and Ralph Carr-Ellison represented the squadron. The George V Jubilee Medal was awarded

607 Squadron group photograph, Usworth, 1938. From left to right: Craig, Glover, Pumphrey, White, Smith, Sqdn Ldr Dunant, Kayll, Turner, Radcliffe, Runciman, Vick, Thompson, Gore, Brotchie (RAF Usworth), Gale, Bazin, Forster, Killick, Irving, Blackadder, Sample, Whitty, Dob Wardale. (Family of John Sample)

Alan Glover at the annual summer camp, 1937. (Family of Dudley Craig)

John Sample – a self-portrait, Warmwell, 1938. (Family of John Sample)

to Sqdn Ldr Runciman and LAC Galbraith. Only two weeks later came the annual summer camp on 20 July, held that year at RAF Manston, Kent. Some twelve officers and eighty-two airmen were to make the trip south to take part. The squadron was paraded in front of Air Commodore J.E.A Baldwin DSO, OBE, and returned north to Usworth on 3 August.

Of course, not all of 607 Squadron's achievements were to come about in the air. The County Durham Rifle Association Battalion Shield was competed for in 1935. This was to bring yet another first to the squadron, when the squadron team won the shield for the first time on 1 September. While the team won the shield, John Sample was to round off the competition by winning the Challenge Cup Individual section. James Michael Bazin from Jesmond, Newcastle upon Tyne, was next to join the squadron, on 9 December. Jim Bazin was another to work in the engineering trade, having worked at the Armstrong Whitworth works at Newcastle upon Tyne. Also joining the squadron during this period was F/O J.S. Bartlett, a regular officer who became the new assistant adjutant. Ralph Carr-Ellison was to leave the squadron temporarily when he was attached to 56 Squadron at North Weald for one month's training, from 22 March 1936, having been promoted to the rank of Flying Officer the previous December.

Jim Bazin. (Family of Francis Blackadder)

John Walton Dobson Wardale, known as 'Dob', was granted a commission as P/O in the accountancy branch on 29 May 1936. Once again, the airfield of Usworth was thrown open to the general public as the aircraft of the day were demonstrated for the Empire Air Day. Crowds of almost 4,000 attended the event, while the amount gathered benefited the RAF Benevolent Fund to the tune of over £127. To round off the month of May, the squadron was invited to the Irish home of the Honorary Commodore, the Marquess of Londonderry, at Newtonards. Five Wapiti aircraft were to make the round trip in one day, the journey interrupted by refuelling at Aldergrove.

The Scottish International rugby player, William Francis Blackadder, was to join the squadron on 1 June 1936. A team representing 607 Squadron travelled to Bisley to take part in the Brooke–Popham–Steele Inter-squadron Challenge Cup. The team consisted of John Sample, Ralph Carr-Ellison, Cpl Hannon and LAC M. Bartley, and were successful on this occasion, carrying off the trophy. The following month was the annual summer camp, which, in this year, took the squadron to RAF Tangmere, an airfield that would feature with some prominence in the later history of 607 Squadron. The summer camp dates had been brought forward due to accommodation difficulties. As a result neither Milne Irving nor Tim Richardson could attend, with F/O S.W. Kaye only making the trip for two days. Aerial gunnery practice was carried out between the 10th and 14th, utilizing the ranges at Lydd. To round off the summer camp, the squadron was given its

J.W.D. (Dob) Wardale and W.B.B.H. (Guff) Griffith, 1939. (Family of Dudley Craig)

inspection by Air Commodore J.C. Quinnell. On their return to Usworth the squadron was to be joined by Flt Lt G.A.L. Manton, known as 'Minnie', a regular RAF officer who became the squadron's new adjutant and flying instructor, taking the place of Flt Lt N.C. Singer, the latter leaving the squadron to pursue an armament course at AAS, RAF Eastchurch.

The squadron was once more to take part in the Durham County Rifle Association Challenge Shield. Having won it the previous year, they were not so lucky the second time, being beaten by a narrow margin. However, all was not lost. LAC Bartley was to tie in the individual trophy and John Sample was to lift the individual revolver trophy, making sure the squadron did not come away empty-handed. It was during this time that the role of the squadron was to change. After being formed and carrying out its duties as a light bomber squadron, 607 Squadron was to take on the mantle of a fighter squadron from 26 September, due to the reforming of the RAF. The Westland Wapiti was to give way to the Hawker Demon, a two-seat fighter derivative of the Hawker Hart. Although officially classed as a fighter squadron, 607 Squadron was to remain with the other Auxiliary Air Force units in Bomber Command. One of the last candidate pilots of the year to be picked was Henry Peter Dixon of Heighington, County Durham. Peter Dixon had first picked up an interest in flying when he had joined the University Air Squadron while he was at Cambridge. He was an engineer and worked with the Cleveland Bridge Company.

In early 1937, two Hawker Harts were flown into Usworth. These were to provide the conversion training for the forthcoming Hawker Demons. Re-equipping the squadron

A portrait of Peter Dixon. (Family of Peter Dixon, via Simon Muggleton)

was carried out swiftly, and the squadron was fully re-equipped by 19 January. Both Launce Smith and Jim Vick were to gain a promotion to the rank of Flight Lieutenant, while F/O S.W. Kaye was transferred to class 'C' reserve when he took up new civil employment that necessitated a move to India. Also on the move was Ralph Carr-Ellison, who departed the squadron when he was attached to 64 Squadron for a month's training. A new trainee pilot to add to the ranks during this period was R.E.W. Pumphrey, known as 'Bobby', gazetted on 19 March 1937. Bobby Pumphrey was one of the true locals, his family roots being in the area of Hylton. An old boy of Sedbergh School and part of the family business, Pumphrey was a keen rugby player. However, he was to be described by his cousin, Harry Welford, who was later to join 607 Squadron, as '… lethargic and spent much of his time reading novels'.[3]

Yet a further change was to come about in early 1937. RAF Usworth had been brought into being to house 607 Squadron and, perhaps one day, a further squadron. That day came on 26 February 1937. 103 Squadron flew into Usworth to become the station's first full-time operational squadron. At first 103 Squadron was commanded by Sqdn Ldr Carey, who was later to relinquish command to Sqdn Ldr Harry Broadhurst. That the world of the RAF was a small place can be seen from two men who shared Usworth during this time, Joe Kayll and Harry Broadhurst. In 1941, Joe Kayll and Harry Broadhurst were to share the command of the Hornchurch Fighter Wing, Joe Kayll as CO flying. This was to have disastrous results for Joe Kayll, who ended up as a PoW. After carrying out a fighter sweep over St Omer, France, Harry Broadhurst insisted

Bobby Pumphrey. (Family of Dudley Craig)

F/O John Sample in a Hawker Demon. (Family of John Sample)

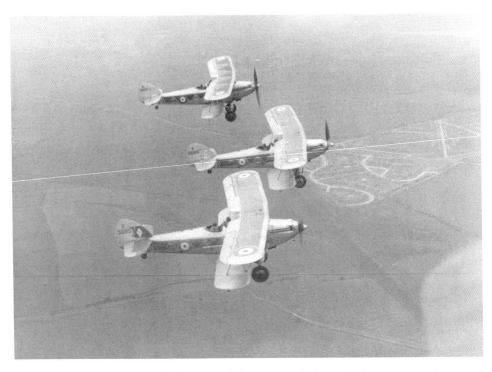

Three Hawker Demons. In the furthest is Will Gore; centre is Tommy Gale; and nearest is Dudley Craig. (Family of Dudley Craig)

Three Demons over Durham countryside. (607 (County of Durham) Squadron Association)

they return for another run. This time they were bounced and Joe Kayll was shot down. 103 Squadron was to fly its sorties during the week, thus leaving the weekends free for the part-timers of 607 Squadron. This was to last for over a year when 103 Squadron departed Usworth in 1938.

The squadron was now seven years old, and it was at this time that it finally gained its official squadron heraldic arms. The badge was described as: 'A winged lion, salient, the hind wings also winged.' Although many attempts were made to give it a motto, none were accepted and the squadron was to remain one of the few squadrons to be without a motto. As with most of the country, the highlight of the year for 607 Squadron was the Coronation of King George VI, and 607 Squadron had its part to play in the event. Francis Blackadder was to depart for London with two NCOs and eight airmen to take part in street-lining duties; they were to appear at Constitution Hill. The following day, Leslie Runciman was to be awarded the AFC in the Coronation Honours for his work in helping to bring 607 Squadron into being. Leslie Runciman had more to celebrate later in the month, when his father, Walter Runciman, was elevated to Viscount Runciman of Doxford. Both Leslie Runciman and Francis Blackadder were awarded the Coronation Medal for their part in the event. Back in the north-east the coronation was celebrated with a military review held on Newcastle's Town Moor. 607 Squadron were called upon to provide the fly-past and the Lord Mayor of Newcastle took the salute. However, after the highs came the gloom. This was caused when one of the squadron's pilots lost his life in a flying accident on 14 May 1937.[4]

Hawker Demons over Sunderland. (Family of Dudley Craig)

A Hawker Demon of 'A' Flight. (Family of Dudley Craig)

Hawker Hart K 6482. (Family of Dudley Craig)

Joe Kayll (left) and Leslie Runciman, Warmwell, 1938. (Family of Dudley Craig)

Tim Richardson, who lived at The Cliffe, Corbridge, Northumberland, elder son of Judge Thomas Richardson, was flying Hawker Demon K5690 on the evening of 14 May. He was almost at the end of his return leg of a cross-country flight from Sutton Bridge, Lincolnshire, when he encountered bad weather off the County Durham coast. In thick fog, he made a landfall to the south of Seaham Harbour. Some twenty to thirty men were gathering sea coal along the beach near Dawdon Colliery when they heard the approach of Richardson's aircraft. The sound of an aeroplane engine was not unusual, but uncommon enough to make the men look up. Martin Loughlin was one of those men gathering sea coal, and on hearing the engine of the aeroplane he looked up and saw it approaching from the sea, flying towards the beach. The aeroplane then changed course and turned south-west towards Hawthorn. Police Constable Atkinson, standing on the cliff top, also noticed the approaching aircraft as it flew towards the cliffs, flying low in the fog before circling the area. He then heard the engine 'racing' before it finally stopped, and the aeroplane then plunged nose first onto the beach near Dawdon Colliery.

It can only be conjecture, of course, trying to work out what happened that night. However, it would appear that Tim Richardson was navigating up the coast of County Durham and made his landfall to the south of Seaham Harbour. In those days navigating was carried out with the use of a map and watch and seat-of-the-pants flying. Approaching the beach near Dawdon Colliery, Richardson began to descend looking for landmarks. He then circled round Dawdon and moved in the direction of Hawthorn, still in a turn, trying to pick up his bearings. It was at this point that Richardson appears to have lost control of his aircraft, and it stalled at low level, leaving him no chance of escape. The Hawker Demon then crashed onto the beach near Dawdon Colliery, only 10 yards from the water's edge. Sidney Horn of nearby Dawdon was in his garden when he heard the aircraft fly over, followed by an explosion, and saw a flash of flame on the beach following this. He ran down to the beach, where he saw the Hawker Demon sticking out of a hole about 4ft deep. Martin Loughlin witnessed the Hawker Demon crash onto the beach in a nosedive, after which it turned over and burst into flames.

The men gathering sea coal than ran to the aid of the pilot but were beaten back by the heat and flames. Still, they could see the pilot so they began to throw sand onto the burning aircraft in an attempt to release the pilot. After about ten minutes of throwing sand on the flames the fire subsided enough to allow them to pull the pilot free. He was already dead. An ambulance arrived on the cliff top, and the men and ambulance crew carried Richardson's body, by means of a precarious path, to the ambulance on the cliff top. The body of Richardson was first taken to the ambulance room at Dawdon Colliery before being transferred to the mortuary at Seaham Harbour. At the inquest some six days later, the verdict given was: 'Death from fracture of the skull and other injuries accidentally received, due to the aeroplane of which he was the pilot, falling to the ground.' Flt Lt G.A.L. Manton was to state that Richardson was an experienced pilot: 'I can only think it was caused by the fog, which left the pilot with no fixed horizon, and, having nothing to go upon, he lost his sense of direction.' Thomas Templar 'Tim' Richardson was buried in Corbridge Cemetery the following Tuesday.

A group at Warmwell, 1938. (Family of Dudley Craig)

Flt Lt George White, Warmwell, 1938. (Family of Dudley Craig)

G.A.L. 'Minny' Manton and Bobby Pumphrey, Austria, 1937. (Family of Dudley Craig)

Bobby Pumphrey, John Humpherson and Launce Smith, Usworth, 1938. (Family of Dudley Craig)

Dudley Craig in Austria. (Family of Dudley Craig)

Although Leslie Runciman was still choosing his pilots carefully, if slowly, new blood was still arriving on the squadron. New arrival George Dudley Craig, known as Dudley Craig, was gazetted on 28 May 1937. Having trained in law he worked in a solicitor's office, and was fairly local to the squadron, living in Hexham, Northumberland. Dudley Craig's first flight is recorded as being in Hawker Hart K6482 on 1 November 1936, the flight being with Flt Lt 'Minnie' Manton.

Alan Otho Glover was not a local, having originated from Runcorn, Cheshire, and was believed to have worked in engineering. He was gazetted as a pilot officer on 4 July 1937. A third new trainee pilot was Montague Henry Brodrick Thompson, known as 'Monty'. He was a former Cambridge student from Newcastle upon Tyne. Monty Thompson had his first flight, an air experience flight, from Usworth in Avro Tutor, K6109, on 9 August with new flying instructor Willy Turner, and was gazetted on 17 August while at summer camp with the squadron. It was during this time that another new pilot arrived on 607 Squadron. John Ryder Hawkes is thought to have been born at Lewes in 1911. He was known to have worked for the London North East Railway and his work may have taken him from England to Scotland. Hawkes was granted a commission as P/O with 602 (City of Glasgow) Squadron on 25 May 1935, and was gazetted on 25 June of that year. His only claim to fame while with 602 Squadron appears to have been that he tipped a Hawker Hart on its nose while making a landing at summer camp in 1937. He was gazetted as having been transferred from 602 Squadron to 607 Squadron on 21 October 1937 (the entry appears in the *London Gazette* issue of 3 November 1937). Departing from the squadron during this time was F/O J.S. Bartlett, assistant adjutant, who moved on to 9 Flying Training School (FTS) Hullavington. Eleven days later he was followed by Flt Lt 'Minnie' Manton, who was posted on to 6 (Auxiliary Group).

Yet another to leave the squadron was Douglas Redington. He departed on 10 November 1937 when he was transferred to 611 (West Lancashire) Squadron, based at Speke, probably due to work commitments. Douglas Redington was not to remain with 611 Squadron for long either. After resigning his commission with the AAF, Douglas Redington was accepted for a short service commission with the RAF. Although the units he served with remain unknown, Douglas Redington had a long service career with the RAF. He was commended for valuable service in the air in 1944 and was gazetted as a Sqdn Ldr on 1 September 1944. Douglas Redington was transferred to the RAF Reserve, with the rank of Flight Lieutenant, on 2 November 1945. He was gazetted on 18 November 1955 as having his service with the Reserve of RAF Officers extended on October 22, 1955. The last known address of Douglas Redington was a farm named East Peterley Manor, Prestwood, in the county of Buckinghamshire.

The annual Empire Air Day was held on 29 May, and in 1937 this was held in conjunction with 103 (B) Squadron, who now shared Usworth with 607 Squadron. Apart from the flying display by aircraft from the two squadrons, a number of visiting aircraft were also to take part and were to add to the open day being a success, with an estimated 15,000 spectators taking in the event. A new assistant adjutant/flying instructor was brought in to replace F/O Bartlett – this was Flt Lt W.H.N. Turner, a former Cranwell cadet known

F/O John Ryder Hawkes (wearing helmet) while he was with 602 (City of Glasgow) Squadron. (Courtesey of 602 (City of Glasgow) Squadron)

Flt Lt W.H.N. (Willy) Turner, Rochford, 1937. (Family of Dudley Craig)

to all on the squadron as Willy. He arrived officially on 28 July 1937.[5] On Sunday 8 August, Leslie Runciman led seven Hawker Demons, carrying some fifteen officers, to Newtonards aerodrome on what was now an annual visit to the home of the Honorary Air Commodore. The Marquess of Londonderry provided a luncheon for the officers at his local seat at Mount Stewart, County Antrim. The seven Hawker Demons returned to Usworth the same day.

Willy Turner was to record that his first flight with 607 Squadron took place on 24 July 1937. This was a routine, local training flight in Hawker Hart, K6482, the flight being with his first pupil, Peter Dixon. The same day he made his first flight in a Hawker Demon, K5689, when he took Bobby Pumphrey on a training flight for some basic flying. His first flight in the squadron's Avro Tutor was with Ralph Carr-Ellison for some instrument flying. Among Willy Turner's regular pupils were Dudley Craig, Tony Glover, Dob Wardale, Monty Thompson, Ralph Carr-Ellison and Francis Blackadder. Willy Turner frequently carried out flights to other airfields – among these was a cross-country flight on 2 August to Hendon with Ralph Carr-Ellison, returning the same day.

As usual it was the annual summer camp that was to provide the highlight of the year for the squadron. The summer camp of 1937 took place at RAF Rochford, near Southend, on 15 August. The unit strength at this time was twenty-three officers and 148 airmen. The squadron aircraft were flown down with the airmen travelling down by road and rail. Willy Turner was to fly down in Avro Tutor K4825, with Monty Thompson as passenger, the aircraft making a stop at RAF Waddington before flying on to Rochford. This year, to simulate war conditions, the officers and airmen were all billeted under canvas with the aircraft picketed. Now part of Fighter Command, the squadron was visited by the Commander in Chief of Fighter Command, Air Marshal Sir Hugh C.T. Dowding, GCVO, KCB, and CMG. The aircraft made good use of the ranges at Eastchurch for air firing practice, while a visit to RAF Hornchurch was arranged for a demonstration of fighter operations and tactics. The Right Honourable Sir Philip Jackson invited the squadron to visit Lympne. Willy Turner records that he made the flight to Lympne in Hawker Demon K5684 with Bobby Pumphrey as a passenger. A sports day was held with the airmen taking part in such activities as a pillow fight. A photograph records this with the officers in the background. On its return to Usworth the squadron broke up for its annual summer break.

Back after its summer break, the squadron, to come into line with other squadrons of Fighter Command, adopted a two-flight system as opposed to its normal three

An informal photograph at the Eldon Grill. (Family of John Sample)

John Sample, Will Gore and Launce Smith at the Eldon Grill. (Family of John Sample)

Joe Kayll (left) and
Bobby Pumphrey in
Austria. (Family of
Dudley Craig)

flights. Now that the squadron was proficient with Hawker Demon during the day, night flying was to be introduced and training for this began on 1 October. When allowed, night flying was carried out in conjunction with the TA searchlight brigades in the area, providing realistic training for both. A different aircraft was to make its appearance at Usworth during November. This was Bristol Blenheim, K8046, which was at Usworth on 12 November. Willy Turner, an ex-bomber pilot, was to record that he gave dual instruction to both Flt Lt 'Minnie' Manton and F/O Rowland. Some of the last training flights of the year, flown by Willy Turner, were recorded as being cross-country flights to Hucknall with the CO, Leslie Runciman: in Hawker Hart K6482 on 3 December, and in Hawker Demon, K5685,[6] with Ralph Carr-Ellison, on 6 December. Only a week later, on 13 December, Ralph Carr-Ellison was to resign his commission with the AAF. The following day he accepted and took up a short service commission with the RAF.[7] Among the air gunners during this time was Charles Edward English; later, he was to be known as 'Honk'. English, a clerk with a Newcastle brewery company, was from the Jesmond area of Newcastle upon Tyne. He is recorded as being a 'passenger' in Demon K8195 when flown on 21 November by Dudley Craig. Charles English was to fly many times with Dudley Craig after this date.[8]

John Sample and Will Whitty. (Family of John Sample)

A portrait of Wilkinson (Vick) Barnes. (Wilkinson Barnes)

Dudley Craig (left) and Willy Turner at Southend, 1937. (Family of Group Captain W.H.N.Turner)

P/O W.H.R. (Nits) Whitty.
(The late Squadron Leader
W.H.R. Whitty)

During the winter months the interviewing of prospective candidate pilots was continued, albeit at a slower pace. As a result more new pilots were to arrive on the squadron. Among these was W.H.R. Whitty, later known as 'Nits'. Will Whitty was from Litherland, on the north side of Liverpool. After studying engineering at Liverpool College and Liverpool University he gained a position with Reyrolle Research in the north-east of England. Whitty appears to have applied to join the Auxiliary Air Force during the winter months of 1937–8, his air experience flights came on 16 January. The first of these was in Hawker Hart, K3040, the second being in Hawker Hart, K4825. Whitty was gazetted as a pilot officer on 17 March 1938. Flt Lt E.T. Smith, assistant adjutant and flying instructor, was to depart at this time for RAF Depot Oxbridge, his place being taken by Flt Lt Tommy G.L. Gale. New pilot Jack A. Killick was gazetted as a pilot officer on 26 March, while A.D. Forster, an ex-Kings' Scholar of Durham School from Bishop Middleham, County Durham, and later known as 'Bunny', had his air experience flight with Willy Turner on 7 April, flying Avro Tutor, K2387. Forster was to be gazetted as a pilot officer on 3 May.

During February, the Lord Esher Trophy was to be fought for. This trophy was awarded to bomber and fighter squadrons of the Auxiliary Air Force on alternate years. In 1938, it was the turn of a fighter squadron. 607 Squadron had been picked to represent 12 Group in the final, their opponents being 604 (County of Middlesex) Squadron representing 11 Group. During the competition both of the squadrons had to get a flight of six aircraft from readiness to attack a formation of five 'enemy' bombers. They then had to return to the airfield, re-arm, refuel, and be ready to go of again. 607 Squadron was not to be successful, however, and was beaten by a narrow margin of seventeen points. The deciding factor lay with the camera-gun film of the attacks, and it was deemed that the film did not show good enough results to allow the squadron to win. At the end of the two days, with the competition over, the Air Officer commanding 12 Group, Air Commodore T.L Leigh-Mallory, visited 607 Squadron.

From 10 January 1938, a number of pilots had flown with Willy Turner towing the 'Drogue', among them Will Gore, Dudley Craig, Jim Vick and Leslie Runciman. Also, to allow the pilots of 607 Squadron to carry out operations against prospective enemy bomber aircraft at higher altitudes, oxygen apparatus was gradually installed in the aircraft from January. To increase the efficiency of both the pilots and air gunners in air firing, a number of aircraft were flown each Sunday, weather permitting, south to 1 Armament Training School, Catfoss, north of Beverley in Yorkshire. The by now annual visit to the Marquess of Londonderry, due to be held on 15 May, had to be cancelled due to the intervention of bad weather. Also during this time, with the Empire Air Day approaching, a number of pilots were engaged in flying activities for the event, particularly formation flying. A photograph exists showing Flt Lt Tommy Gale leading Dudley Craig and Will Gore, the aircraft being Hawker Demons, K5688, K5685 and K3800, as they fly over the County Durham countryside. Willy Turner was also to note that he was engaged in formation flying practice, flying in Hawker Hart, K6428, with AP/O Strong. As for the Empire Day itself, it was to have less success than in previous years, with most of the flying programme having to be curtailed due to the bad weather.

Although gazetted on 11 July, new pilot candidate Harry Radcliffe was already receiving flying instructionearlier in the year when he was flying Avro Tutor, K2387, on 24 April with Willy Turner. Harry Peter Joseph Radcliffe was the elder son of Sir Everard Joseph, 5th Bt, KCSG, JP, and Lady Radcliffe, formerly Marguerite Magdalene Ashton Case of Richmond, Yorkshire. Harry was known to have worked on the London Stock Exchange before he took to flying. Oddly, he is not mentioned on the Radcliffe family tree which can be viewed on the internet. Upon the death of his father, Harry's brother, Joseph Benedict Everard Henry Radcliffe, became 6th Bt. Also receiving flying training during this time was Wilkinson Barnes, another 'old boy' of Durham School turned estate agent from Sunderland, known as 'Vick'. Barnes was to be gazetted on 2 August while at summer camp.

Prior to the annual summer camp, a command exercise was to be held at Catterick, Yorkshire, over the weekend of 18–19 June. The exercise was to consist of demonstrations, practices, bombing raids and fighter interceptions. The whole exercise was to be held in conjunction with 41 Squadron and 608 (Thornaby) Squadron. The squadron's annual summer camp of 1938 was held at Warmwell, Dorset. As usual, all squadron aircraft were ferried down while the airmen travelled by road and rail. Willy Turner flew Hawker Hart K6467 to Warmwell, stopping off at Hucknall and Upavon. This year, the summer camp

'Guff' Griffith. (Family of Dudley Craig)

was to be shared with 504 (City of Nottingham) Squadron and 605 (County of Warwick) Squadron. Emphasis during this camp, as far as the squadron was concerned, focused on air-to-air and air-to-ground firing. Meanwhile, visits to the squadron were made by two VIPs; first was the Under Secretary of State for Air, Captain H.H. Balfour MC, MP, who made his visit on 5 August, while the Secretary of State for Air, the Rt Hon. Sir Kingsley Wood MP, made his visit on 9 August. With the summer camp over and the squadron back at Usworth, there was tension and a feeling that something was about to happen, and so it did – the whole squadron was embodied into the RAF. This was due to a complicated situation which had arisen, the squadron being assimilated from 2 a.m. on that date. Jim Vick and one airman could not report for duty due to illness, while a further two airmen were abroad. All of the airmen were to be billeted in the station and squadron huts, and the whole embodiment was completed with the squadron ready for action by 30 September. However, no further order was given to mobilise and all training was carried out as normal. With the international situation calming down once more, the squadron was again disembodied as of 11 October.

The events leading up to the embodiment of 607 Squadron had their beginnings earlier that year. Hitler made it quite clear that his intention was to occupy the Sudetenland, an area of Czechoslovakia populated principally by German settlers, and this was unacceptable to Britain, France, the USSR and Czechoslovakia itself. However, Hitler made it quite clear that if he could not do this, then he would occupy the whole of Czechoslovakia. In a quirk of fate, the man sent to assess into the situation was Walter Runciman,

AOC's annual inspection of camouflaged Hawker Demons, 1938. (Family of Dudley Craig)

Flt Lt Tommy Gale, 1938. (Family of Dudley Craig)

First Viscount Runciman of Doxford and father of Leslie Runciman, CO of 607 Squadron. The situation worsened and Hitler used the threat to invade Czechoslovakia as political leverage. The threat led to the mobilisation of the British forces in the expectation that war was imminent. A meeting between Britain, Germany, Italy and France, with Czechoslovakia and the USSR excluded, brought about the famous 'piece of paper' leading to Chamberlain declaring 'peace in our time'. Chamberlain was hailed as a hero by some while Czechoslovakia and the USSR denounced his work as appeasement, as Hitler was given the Sudetenland. British forces were once again disembodied as the pressure was removed. At a later date, of course, events were to dramatically change as the German forces invaded Poland. Hitler was to deride the peace agreement as nothing more than a 'piece of paper'. It was at this time that the uneasy peace created the conditions for the Second World War. Although this event must have had more than a little effect on 607 Squadron and its personnel, the logbook of Dudley Craig fails to make any mention of embodiment or disembodiment.

Harry Welford was to join the squadron around this time. He had first been introduced to the squadron and given an air experience flight by his cousin, Bobby Pumphrey, in 1938. During the flight, Harry Welford had been sick due to Bobby Pumphrey indulging in some light aerobatics and pulling a loop. Harry Welford was still under training, studying to be an engineer with the Armstrong Whitworth works in Newcastle upon Tyne, as well as studying at Durham University. His application, therefore, had been put on hold for a year. Harry Welford states that he joined 607 Squadron in November of 1938 citing a diary extract of 4 December 1938: '... have been accepted for training.'[9] He also states that his first flying instructor was Tommy Gale. However, he is noted as flying in Avro Tutor W3407 on basic flying, when his instructor was Willy Turner. Now, in the winter months, more emphasis was placed on night flying training. Among those given dual night flying training with Willy Turner were: Jim Bazin, Francis Blackadder, Will Whitty and Tony Forster. All flew in Hawker Hart K6482.

It was somewhat ironic that just as the training was stepped up on the Hawker Demon, the squadron was notified that they were to re-equip with the Gloster Gladiator, a single-seat fighter and the most modern on the squadron so far, but still a biplane. For the first time the squadron was to fly single-seat aircraft, with the result that its air gunners were now surplus to requirements. The air gunners were therefore given three choices: 1) apply for pilot training; 2) re-muster under another trade; or 3) apply for a free discharge. Two were immediately picked for pilot training while a third was placed under consideration.[10]

The reign of Leslie Runciman as squadron commander came to an end on 1 January 1939. On this date he was appointed to the general list. On the same day, Flt Lt Launce Smith was moved up to acting squadron leader and appointed commanding officer of 607 Squadron. Both Joe Kayll and John Sample were promoted to the rank of Flight Lieutenant, with John Sample appointed as Flight Commander of 'B' Flight. Meanwhile, Jack Killick was transferred from flying to armament duties on 4 February, and on 2 October he was posted to RAF Manby. Also leaving the squadron was Willy Turner. On 6 February Willy Turner managed to squeeze in a flight in Gladiator K7982, for air practice. This was to be the last flight Willy Turner was to make with 607 Squadron, as he left that same day to join 51 Squadron as (B) Flight Commander. His place on the squadron was taken by Tommy Gale, who moved up from assistant adjutant, while P/O W.B.B.H. Griffiths arrived from the Central Flying School (CFS) to take over as assistant adjutant.

It was during this time that Harry Welford was to describe an incident with one of the squadron's Gladiators. A Gladiator had made a forced landing in a field near Shildon Colliery. Tommy Gale, on a training flight with Harry Welford, decided to check the length of the field for suitability for the Gladiator take-off. However, lifting off from the field, the Avro Tutor hit the top of the hedge and was tipped onto its back. The Gladiator was known to be K6149, which had arrived at 607 Squadron on 5 January 1939, having been formerly on charge with 25 Squadron. On 6 February 1939, it was being flown by an unnamed pilot, when its engine cut out and a forced landing was carried out in a field near Shildon Colliery. However, during the landing a tyre burst as well and the Gladiator was damaged. The Gladiator was eventually returned to 607 Squadron after repairs had been carried out by 1 Repair and Servicing Depot. To facilitate the removal, both aircraft had to be dismantled and returned to Usworth by road.

The re-equipment of the squadron with the Gladiator was completed by the end of March. Initially pilots almost had to queue to get a flight in the new arrival. Dudley Craig was to get his first flight in the aircraft on 8 January, when he flew Gladiator K8030 on circuits and landings.[11] Gazetted on 26 February was Stewart Parnall, his air experience flight having taken place the previous June. Stewart Parnall, like most of the other squadron pilots, was an ex-public schoolboy who had spent a number of years as an estate manager on a Malayan rubber plantation. The Empire Air Day was held on 20 May. Unknown to participants and spectators alike, this was to be the last. The Air Show proved to be up to the usual standard of the years before, with many aircraft in the ground exhibits while a number of various planes took part in the flying display, including a visit by an aircraft which was soon to be well known: the Spitfire. The set piece on the ground was the attack and defence of positions on the airfield. Dudley Craig was to note that he flew Gladiator K7999 in the dive bombing attacks that took place in front of a crowd numbering around 13,500. 2 June 1939 saw the end of tenure for the Honorary Air Commodore, Lord Londonderry. Filling his place was the former commanding officer of 607 Squadron, Leslie Runciman, who was also promoted to the rank of Wing Commander. Four pilots also came to the end of their initial service with the Auxiliary Air Force. These were: Jim Vick, Joe Kayll, John Sample and Will Gore, all of which immediately extended their length of service. In addition, Joe Kayll volunteered to take an instructor's course, with the result that he was attached to the Central Flying School (CFS) for two weeks' training from 1–15 July. A further two departures took place during this time. Milne Irving was transferred to reserve Class 'A' and moved south to Slough, presumably employment orientated. P/O W.B.B.H. Griffiths, assistant adjutant, was posted to RAF Cranwell as a flying instructor from 8 August.

The summer camp of 1939 was to be held at Abbotsinch near Glasgow, home of 602 (City of Glasgow) Squadron. As usual, the aircraft were flown to the camp while the airmen travelled by road and rail transport. The flying party flew up the coast of Northumberland and eastern Scotland before turning west to Abbotsinch by way of

RAF Turnhouse. The Gladiators were flown up in squadron formation whilst the training aircraft followed up in open order. There were two Demons, two Hart trainers, three Tutors and a Moth, the latter formation being led by the instructors. Harry Welford was to note that this was '… the longest cross country I had done'.[12] The only mishap on the whole flight was when Francis Blackadder made a heavier than usual landing, but without any damage. The first Sunday of a summer camp was traditionally a day for attending church. However, a small group, namely Joe Kayll, Jim Bazin, Peter Dixon, Will Gore, Tony Glover and Dudley Craig, decided that a day out to Rowardennan and a climb up Ben Lomond would be better.[13] The last 200ft of Ben Lomond were fought over between Tony Glover and Jim Bazin. This was followed on the descent by a swim in the ice cool waters of a private watering hole they had spotted on the way up. The whole trip was rounded off with a stop at the Buchanan Arms at Drymen. Both Joe Kayll and Tony Glover then gave an impromptu gymnastic display down the pathway.

After the interlude at Ben Lomond, the squadron got down to the more serious training. Fine weather, particularly during the first week, allowed the emphasis to be on air firing, and this was carried out in the vicinity of Ailsa Craig. The final group photographs of the squadron were taken, one showing the full squadron and another showing the pilots only. Seated on the front row of the latter was Willy Turner, at this time with 51 Squadron at RAF Dishforth. Willy Turner seems to have made a clandestine trip to Abbotsinch – he is not mentioned in the squadron ORB and there is no entry in his logbook. Two visits were made to the squadron during their stay at Abbotsinch. The first was by Air Vice Marshal R.E. Saul DFC, AOC 13 Group, on 18 August, and the second by Air Commodore H. Peake, director of the Auxiliary Air Force, who visited on 22 August. The following afternoon, instructions were received that the Auxiliary Air Force was to be embodied into the RAF. Equipment and stores were packed as the summer camp came to an abrupt end, and 607 Squadron departed Abbotsinch for Usworth on 24 August. The journey, made with a mixed feeling of sombreness as well as excitement, took the westerly route travelling by way of Carlisle. Those who travelled by rail arrived at Usworth by 9.30 p.m. All were immediately embodied into the RAF and those who had not attended were sent call-up papers. On arrival at Usworth, the squadron was met with the site of manned machine gun posts and personnel dressed in anti-gas regalia. 607 Squadron was now to prepare for what it had trained for: war.

Notes

1. Wynn, *Men of The Battle of Britain*, p.319, states that McComb joined 611 Squadron from 600 Squadron, and fails to mention he had been with 607 Squadron.
2. 607 Squadron ORB.
3. Welford, *The Unrelenting Years 1916–46*, p.24.
4. Tim Richardson was caught in fog when he neared the Durham coast. It is thought that he became disorientated and his aircraft had stalled and fell onto the beach. Men picking sea coal threw sand on the aircraft to put out the fire and they also pulled his body free. *Newcastle Journal*, 15 and 21 May.

5. Logbook of Willy Turner, in which he states that his first flight with 607 Squadron was a training flight with Peter Dixon in Hawker Hart K6482. This flight took place on 24 July.

6. Logbook of Willy Turner.

7. Theodore Ralph Tate Carr-Ellison was later to serve with 54 Squadron. While flying Gladiator K7930 of that squadron from Hornchurch on 26 January, in a snow-storm, he flew into the ground near Baldock, Hertfordshire. He died in Letchworth Hospital, Hertfordshire, on 30 January 1939. He was later buried at Brainshaugh, Northumberland. He has no stone and is buried within the vault of his mother's family, the Tate family, within the ruined priory of Brainshaugh.

8. Logbook of Dudley Craig states that English was his passenger.

9. Welford, p.86.

10. 607 Squadron ORB. Possibly these were Wilkinson Barnes, Charles E. English and Herbert Cottam.

11. Logbook of Dudley Craig.

12. Welford, p.92.

13. From records by Major J.H. Dixon on his brother Peter Dixon. In possession of the Dixon family.

CHAPTER THREE

TOWARDS WAR

On 24 August 1939, 607 Squadron had departed their summer camp at Abbotsinch. Their days of training were now behind them and ahead the real thing was about to start. 607 Squadron would be in the action as a fighter squadron within 13 Fighter Group. This the pilots knew, as their role would be the air defence of Sunderland and part of the north-east of England. Just how much bigger an area they would have to cover they did not yet know. Already the squadron aircraft were looking different. They had been camouflaged in green and brown before departing on summer camp. Now, in line with other squadrons in the RAF, the squadron code letters were changed in an effort to confuse German Intelligence. Gone was the old LW, to be replaced by the new AF. The squadron pilots were sent home, on what they thought may be their last chance for leave for some time, and in order to take leave of their full-time employment, as they were now no longer just part-time flyers.

September brought the news that everyone knew was inevitable. At 11 a.m. on Sunday 3 September 1939, Prime Minister Neville Chamberlain announced that Britain was now at war with Germany. The training at Usworth was to increase with the news of war, not only for the regular pilots but also for those still under training. Harry Welford managed to squeeze in four or five extra solo trips in the squadron's Avro Tutor. Later in the month he was taken aloft by Joe Kayll, as a senior pilot on the squadron. Joe Kayll was also a training officer. Harry Welford also managed to add a few hours' dual flying in the squadron's Hawker Hart. Wanting to cram in as much flying training as possible, Harry Welford added a night flight in a Hawker Demon to his list. In his biography, Harry Welford fails to name the pilot of the Demon on this flight, probably with good cause considering how the flight went. For some reason, again unspecified, the pilot of the Demon carried out a loop. For Harry Welford, it was all part of the excitement of flying, until they returned to Usworth. When he began to unstrap himself from the cockpit, Harry Welford was shocked to find his safety harness had not been secured. All that had held Harry Welford in the cockpit, during the display of aerobatics, was gravity and his own hands. Had Harry Welford released his grip on the cockpit sides, he would have shot out like a cork and been no more.[1]

The pilots of 607 Squadron, called back from summer camp, were expecting a war situation and were eager to get on with it – maybe a little too eager. At around 10 p.m. on the

607 Squadron at Abbotsinch in 1939, the last group photograph before the Second World War. Rear, from left to right: Welford, Craig, Parnall, Pumphrey, Whitty, Griffith, Weatherill, Glover, Radcliffe, Forster, Barnes, Thompson, Dixon. Front, left to right: Blackadder, Bazin, -?-, Sample, Gale, Smith, Turner, Kayll, White, Gore, Dob Wardale. (Family of Dudley Craig)

The full squadron group, Abbotsinch, 1939. (Family of Dudley Craig)

night of 3 September, only two days after war had been officially declared, three members of 'A' flight were on patrol, in the defence of their home of Sunderland – as they saw it. Red section, consisting of Will Gore, Francis Blackadder and Peter Dixon, were on the 'South patrol line searching for the enemy'.[2] For forty minutes Red Section patrolled the area, seeing nothing but distant flashes which could have been anything. However, there was no sign of the enemy and Red Section returned to Usworth a little disappointed. This was to be the first operational patrol of the war for 607 Squadron.

The squadron was in a state of flux during this time as members departed and others arrived. Among those to leave was Tommy Gale, flying instructor and adjutant, promoted from Flight Lieutenant to Squadron Leader. He now departed the squadron for RAF Records at Ruislip. Moved into his place was Flt Lt George White, a non-flying member of the squadron who had been involved in administration duties since joining the squadron in 1935. An 'old hand' returning to the squadron was Milne Irving, newly returned from the south. He had been recalled from the reserve list, arriving back on the squadron on 24 September 1939.

Another experienced pilot to arrive on the squadron was F/O J.W.B. Humpherson, transferred from SHQ Usworth. John Humpherson was born in Enfield, Middlesex, in 1916. He was later educated at Brighton College and joined the RAF on a short service commission. After passing through 10 Flying Training School (FTS) he was posted to 32 Squadron in August 1937. He was later posted to SHQ Usworth and subsequently 607 Squadron, on 10 October 1939. However, as the new faces arrived on the squadron,

The group on No.12 course: 7 FTS Peterborough, 1939. (607 (County of Durham) Squadron Association)

H.W. 'Bert' Cottam. (Maurice Cottam)

some of the others had to depart. The trainee pilots, their training uncompleted, were ordered to 7 Flying Training School (FTS) at Peterborough for completion of their flying training. Among those departing were Harry Welford, LAC Sydenham, Bert Cottam and Charles English. Of those four, one was fêted to return while the others were to move on to other squadrons.

Harry Welford was to make a return to 607 Squadron in time for the Battle of Britain. Hubert Weatherby Cottam, known as 'Bert', was an ex-Bede Grammar School boy from Sunderland. He had been head boy at the school as well as the assistant scoutmaster for the Bede Troop. On leaving school, Cottam had worked in the offices of the Newcastle-based company Northern Assurance. Cottam had joined 607 Squadron as an aircraft hand in 1938 and later applied for pilot training. In the latter part of 1938, Bert Cottam had re-mustered into the RAFVR and was posted to 7 FTS at Peterborough for further flying training.

Bert Cottam was commissioned on 21 March 1940 and was posted to 6 OTU at Sutton Bridge for conversion onto the Hawker Hurricane, after which he was posted to 213 Squadron on 25 May. 213 Squadron was later to fly from Tangmere during the latter part of the Battle of Britain. It was during this time that Cottam suffered a minor injury when his Hurricane was riddled with bullets from a Me 109. Cottam was sent on an instructor's course in the latter part of 1940 and it was as a flying instructor that he was sent to Rhodesia, serving with 23 SFTS at Heany. It is thought that Cottam was instructing on Oxfords when the Oxford he was flying in crashed and he was killed. Bert Cottam was buried in Bulawayo Cemetery, Zimbabwe, grave 25.

Charles Edward English was born in 1912 to Joseph and Bertha E. English, the eldest of three children. His family lived in the Jesmond area of Newcastle upon Tyne. Charles English, later known as 'Honk', worked in the offices of Newcastle Brewery. He is thought to have been a member of Newcastle Aero Club based at Woolsington, now Newcastle Airport, and is known to have been on 607 Squadron from 1937. He was recorded as flying with Dudley Craig on 21 November 1937, when he flew on two flights as an air gunner in Hawker Demon K5685. Prior to that he had flown with Francis Blackadder when he flew in Hawker Demon K5683 on 24 October 1937, during which they took part in a battle climb. Charles English travelled the same training route as Bert Cottam. However, Charles English was posted to 85 Squadron, then working up and training its new pilots under their new commanding officer, Peter Townsend, at Debden.

Charles English, along with 85 Squadron, was heavily involved in the Battle of Britain during July and August. He flew regularly as number two to either Peter Townsend or Sammy Allard, whoever was leading the squadron that day. In early September, 85 Squadron was withdrawn from the Battle of Britain for a rest. However, Charles English was a battle-experienced pilot, and squadrons in the 'battle' were short of experienced men; Charles English, therefore, was posted to 605 (County of Warwick) Squadron based at Croydon. On 4 October 1940, Charles English was involved in an inconclusive dog-fight with Me 109s. His Hurricane, V6784, UP-E, sustained damage that forced its pilot to look for a quick landing. This was carried out in a field on Pitchfont Farm near Keymer to the north of Brighton, around 4.55 p.m.

7 October saw a break in the weather and 605 Squadron were involved in heavy fighting over Westerham around 1.20 p.m. Hurricane P3677 was shot down by Me 109s, probably JG 27, and crashed onto land at Park Farm, Brasted, killing its pilot, Charles English. Peter Townsend, shot down shortly before 85 Squadron was withdrawn from the battle, stated that he thought he had lost his fighting edge. Charles English had been flying for the same amount of time as Peter Townsend – perhaps he too had lost his edge. The remains of Charles English were transported north to Newcastle, where he was buried in the family grave in St Andrews and Jesmond Cemetery. He also shares the grave with his brother, Robin, also killed as a fighter pilot while flying with 3 Squadron in 1941.

Neville Charles Langham-Hobart was born at Tynemouth in 1912, one of two children born to Frank and Hilda Daisy Langham-Hobart. The family was known to have lived in the Jesmond area of Newcastle upon Tyne. Although little is known of his early life, Neville Langham-Hobart is known to have attended Newcastle Grammar School. It is thought the he joined 607 Squadron around August 1939, although he was not to remain on the squadron for long, as he was posted to 7 FTS at Peterborough for further flying training. Langham-Hobart was gazetted as a pilot officer on 7 March 1940. Wynn states that he was next posted to 611 Squadron, a Spitfire squadron. However, this may be inaccurate as Neville Langham-Hobart was known to have joined 73 Squadron, a Hurricane squadron based at Rouvres in France, on 11 May 1940. There would hardly have been time to convert to both types of aircraft in that time.

It was during his time with 73 Squadron that Neville Langham-Hobart became known as 'Hangman' Hobart. On 19 May, 73 Squadron attacked a German formation and during the ensuing dogfight the Hurricane of Langham-Hobart was seen to fall away from the fighting. Although badly damaged, the Hurricane made a 'wheels-up' landing and Langham-Hobart suffered only two bruised knees. After the downfall of France, 73 Squadron returned to England, where the squadron was posted to Church Fenton to rest and rebuild the squadron.

73 Squadron were to return south on 5 September, and were to suffer heavy losses. 23 September saw a large formation approaching the English coast, and once more 73 Squadron were to suffer – one of those shot down was Hurricane L2036, that of Langham-Hobart. Although the Hurricane was on fire, Langham-Hobart chose to stay with his aircraft. On this occasion he was to pay dearly. His Hurricane ditched near Lightship 93 in the Thames Estuary. In the attempted ditching, Langham-Hobart was severely burned. Picked up by the Royal Navy, he was admitted to the Royal Navy Hospital at Chatham before being passed on to the Queen Victoria Hospital at East Grinstead, where he became one of Sir Archibald McIndoes 'guinea pigs'.

Langham-Hobart was later posted to the Ministry of Aircraft production before being posted to Canada. While there he took a specialist navigational course before he began instructing at Charlotte Town, Prince Edward Island. On his return to the UK, Hobart was posted to HQ 13 Fighter Group, Newcastle. The rest of his RAF career was spent in navigational posts both in the UK and overseas. Langham-Hobart was released from RAF service in September 1945 with the rank of Squadron Leader. He died at his home in Ponteland, Northumberland, in September 1994 and he was cremated at the West Road Crematorium, Newcastle upon Tyne. Of the other fledgling flyers from 607 Squadron, Frank Sydenham and J.E.P. Thompson, there appears to be no trace. A group photograph of 12 Course at No 7 FTS remains in existence as the only evidence of what these men looked like.

Changes were due to be made to Usworth itself. A modernisation plan was underway to bring Usworth up to the standard of a front-line fighter station befitting Usworth's war station capabilities within 13 Fighter Group. Airfield defences as well as ancillary buildings had to be erected. However, one of the largest undertakings was the building of a concrete runway, the grass version deemed to be no longer suitable. The work and all it entailed would render Usworth unusable as a fighter station in the short-term. A new airfield had to be found, but where? There was only one place suitable: RAF Acklington in Northumberland. The squadron would still be based in the North East as part of the air defence of that region. To the members of the squadron, it was not that far away from their traditional home and, therefore, no major hardship. In reality, Acklington was, and still is, set in a bleak landscape. Future pilots, on being posted to Acklington, would look on it as the 'back of beyond', a last outpost. To the pilots of 607 Squadron, however, it was still home and not too far removed from their traditional home. On Tuesday 10 October 1939, sixteen Gloster Gladiators of 607 Squadron flew into Acklington after a short flight from Usworth. The squadron was to join the resident 609 (Spitfire) and 152 Squadrons, also flying Gladiators. However, air defence duties for Acklington fell mainly to 607 Squadron, as 152 Squadron was not operational and 609 Squadron was operational

The sports group at Abbotsinch. From the left at the front are Joe Kayll and Alan Glover. On the far right, three from the front, is Jim Bazin. (Family of Francis Blackadder/Family of John Sample)

Group shot at Abbotsinch, 1939. From left to right: Bobby Pumphrey, Francis Blackadder, Joe Kayll, Alan Glover, John Sample and Jim Bazin. (Family of John Sample)

Ben Lomond. From left to right: Peter Dixon, Joe Kayll, Dudley Craig, Jim Bazin and Alan Glover. (Family of Dudley Craig)

A trip to Ben Lomond. From left to right: Alan Glover, Joe Kayll, Peter Dixon, Dudley Craig and Jim Bazin. (Family of Dudley Craig)

for daylight flying only. 607 Squadron was fully operational, by night and day, as soon as they touched down at Acklington.

It was during October 1939 that Joe Kayll was to clock up his 1,000th hour of flying. This, of course, had to be celebrated in the traditional way. A party was organized at Foxton Hall Golf Club. The party of pilots did their level best to drink the place dry. On leaving, and still in the party mood, they next moved to The Ship Inn at Alnmouth to repeat the performance. The party now over, they set out for Acklington. However, there appeared to be one or two extra corners on the way, causing the car to leave the road. While all the occupants of the car were to show signs of scratches and shock, it was Will Gore who was to cause the most shock to the group. Propelled from his seat like a cork from a bottle, Will Gore lay inert on the grass. Luckily, the tension was released when Will Gore sat up and '… giving vent to a satisfying and expressive oath',[3] was back in the land of the living. The party, somewhat subdued after their adventure, returned to Acklington under their own steam. The next day they returned to the scene of the accident, firstly to recover their car, and secondly to recover their hats, which they found all in a line on top of the hedge.

16 October brought a change in the routine. Orders were received at 12.45 p.m. that the whole squadron was to proceed to Drem, East Lothian. The move was brought about by suspected enemy air activity around the Firth of Forth. After a thirty-minute flight, 607 Squadron landed at Drem. Distinct and heavy anti-aircraft fire was heard by squadron members and the whole squadron was put on readiness – this was followed by the order to scramble. Red Section, comprising Joe Kayll, Alan Glover and Tony Forster, were followed by Yellow Section: Will Gore, Francis Blackadder and Peter Dixon, with Blue and Green Sections taking up the rear. The squadron patrolled the area of Drem and the Firth of Forth at 10,000ft. However, the only evident action came from HMS *Mohawk*, who, for some reason, took a dislike to the Gladiators of 607 Squadron. Will Gore was later to state that every time HMS *Mohawk* opened fire, he got sensation of 'lift'.

607 Squadron was unlucky on this day. The reason that HMS *Mohawk* had appeared to be 'trigger happy' was the fact that ships in the Firth of Forth were under attack from Ju 88s of KG 30. While 607 Squadron flew at 10,000ft, the Ju 88s, courtesy of a power failure that put the radar out of action, were allowed to approach their targets undetected at low level. It was left to 603 Squadron from Turnhouse to gain the first victory of the war, as a Ju 88 flopped into the sea of Port Seton. Yet another was chased at rooftop height across Mussleborough, causing houses to be hit by the gunfire of the pursuing Spitfires. This Ju 88 proved to have luck on his side, because although one engine was out of action it managed to escape. For the pilots of 607 Squadron, four patrols had left them with no action against the enemy, and they were forced to curse their luck and take the odd kick at an undercarriage wheel. At 11 p.m. the squadron was given the order to return to Acklington at dawn the next day. Even the ground crews had been cursed with a bad day. They had only arrived at Drem at 8.30 p.m., after suffering a severe delay due to a traffic accident.

As 607 Squadron returned to Acklington from Drem, two Dornier Do 18 flying boats of 2/KuFlrGr 606 left their base at Sylt at around 7 a.m. Normally their patrol area took

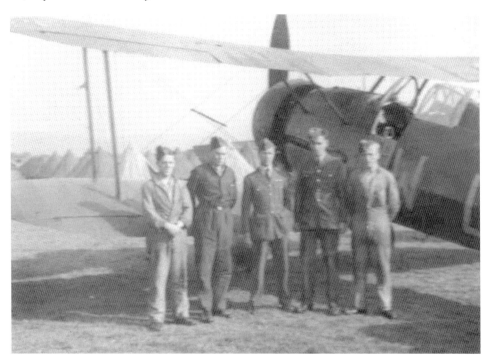

Dudley Craig with 'B' Flight ground crew, Abbotsinch, 1939. (Family of Dudley Craig)

'B' Flight ground crew, Abbotsinch, 1939.

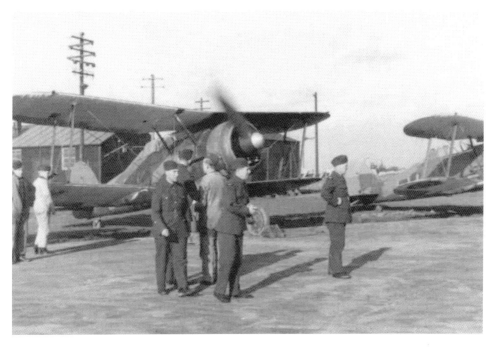

Gloster Gladiators of 607 Squadron. (Family of Dudley Craig)

The cockpit of Dudley Craig's Gladiator 'L'. (Family of Dudley Craig)

Will Gore, 1939. (Family of Dudley Craig)

them up the coast to Norway, but on this day their route was to differ, taking them across the North Sea to the area off the Firth of Forth. The flight was a general reconnaissance, mainly checking on the Royal Naval shipping in and around the Firth of Forth. During the raid in that area the day before, the Luftwaffe had lost some aircraft; the Do 18s had been detailed to look for these and, if possible, pick up their crews. Do 18 8L+DK was flown by Fwb Grabbet. Alongside him, acting as observer, was the commander of the aircraft: Oblt Zur See Siegfried Saloga. Behind them, in his radio cabin, sat Unfwb Hilmar Grimm, who was radio operator as well as acting observer. Completing the crew was Uffz Seydel, who manned the rearward-firing gun. The trip was made in company with Do 18 8L+AK, flown by their Flight Commander, Hptmn Wodarg, the two aircraft flying in a wide search formation, just keeping each other in sight.

The flight was routine until the aircraft approached the Isle of May off the Fife coast. It was at this point that the aircraft came under heavy, concentrated and accurate fire from the Destroyer HMS *Juno*, still on high alert after the air raids of the previous day. Deciding discretion was the better part of valour, Hptmn Wodarg turned the flight south, flying down the east coast of Scotland and Northumberland. At around 12.40 p.m., Blue Section of 'B' Flight, consisting of Dudley Craig, AF-L, and Will Whitty, led by John Sample AF-O, was ordered off from RAF Acklington to look for enemy seaplane activity. The three Gladiators flew on a bearing of 100°, climbing to a patrol altitude of 10,000ft, taking them to a point some 25 miles off the port of Blyth with a view covering the approaches of the River Tyne. With nothing seen, John Sample turned the section in a northerly direction. However, nearing the end of their patrol, the section was about to turn for home when below, through a break in the clouds, an aircraft was spotted. The aircraft turned out to be a flying boat of enemy-type. John Sample ordered the section to dive on the enemy flying boat some 8,000ft below.

The Do 18 spotted was that of Fwb Grabbet. In the mid-upper section, Uffz Seydel was the first to spot the descending Gladiators and called out the warning as he readied himself for the attack. Fwb Grabbet put the Do 18 into a steep dive that took the aircraft down to 50ft above the sea, then descending down to 20ft, denying the Gladiators a good shot from under the vulnerable tail of the Do 18. John Sample called his section into line astern and each of the Gladiators made three passes on the Do 18. Pieces were seen by all the pilots to be flying off the Do 18. Will Whitty noticed fuel escaping from a wing tank and panels missing as he made one of his attacks.[4] The Do 18 was still determined that it could make good on its escape, and Will Whitty noticed that it almost 'put a wing in' as Fwb Grabbet pulled a steep, low-level turn. However, by now the Gladiators had expended all their ammunition, and with their fuel also running low, they had to turn for home. The three pilots could only watch with disappointment as the Do 18, trailing smoke and fuel, limped off in the opposite direction. Slightly zig-zagging, it gave the impression of a wounded animal looking for a place to die.

However, aboard the Do 18 things were not so well. After Uffz Seydel called out his warning of the impending attack he swung his gun in the direction of the oncoming fighters. In the first burst of gunfire, Uffz Seydel fell dead on the floor of the Do 18. The rear of the Do 18 was now unprotected, and Will Whitty reported that the return fire was ineffective at this time. When the bullets began to fly, Unfwb Hilmar Grimm threw himself on the floor of the radio cabin seeking sanctuary beneath the Do 18's engines. Fwb Grabbet gamely tried to elude the attacking fighters, even though he had been wounded in the arm. Oblt Zur See Siegfried Saloga had also been shot in the leg as well as having facial wounds. As the Do 18 limped northwards, Fwb Grabbet contacted Hptmn Wodarg in the second Do 18; mysteriously this second Do 18 had not been spotted by the Gladiators and remained undetected.

Now the Do 18s were some 40 miles to the north-east of Berwick, and Fwb Grabbet decided he could go no further. With the help of Unfwb Hilmar Grimm, who worked the throttles, Fwb Grabbet landed the Do 18. The intention was for the Do 18 of Hptmn Wodarg to rescue the crew of the other Do 18. However, the plan went wrong when it was found that the rubber dinghy of Grabbet's aircraft had been damaged in the attack. A previous SOS sent out by Hilmar Grimm had not only alerted the accompanying Do 18 of Hptmn Wodarg, but had also been picked up by HMS *Juno*, the latter now moving to the area at high speed. As Hptmn Wodarg's crew contemplated the rescue, the accurate gunfire from HMS *Juno* hurried the decision. Knowing that at least their comrades would be rescued, Hptmn Wodarg departed the scene.

HMS *Juno* closed in on the Do 18 and took the crew prisoner.[5] The stricken Do 18 had a line attached and was towed behind the Destroyer as it turned northwards, until the plane eventually sank. It is probable that the Do 18 crew were put ashore at the port of Leith, as Uffz Seydel was buried at Mussleborough. The three remaining crew members were kept apart. After having his arm amputated, Fwb Grabbet[6] would only admit to

Gloster Gladiators at Abbotsinch, 1939. (Family of Dudley Craig)

A Dornier Do 18. Photography was much used by the press of the day. This was the aircraft shot down by Navy fighters on 26 September 1939. (Family of John Sample)

the interrogating officer that they had been 'joy riding'. Oblt Zur See Siegfried Saloga admitted to being 'disappointed at becoming a PoW', while Unfwb Hilmar Grimm gave a statement providing us with the German side of what happened that day. The three Gladiators returned to Acklington at 2.10 p.m., slightly dejected that the Do 18 had got away. However, news came through at about 7 p.m. that the Do 18 had come down and the crew made PoWs. The three pilots were awarded a ⅓ share of the 'kill' each. Dudley Craig was to write of the event that, 'This was Johnnie's work', a reference to the leadership of John Sample.

There would appear to have been a flurry of enemy activity on this day, especially of the flying boat type. No sooner had Blue Section returned to Acklington than another section was ordered off. On this occasion it was Bobby Pumphrey and Monty Thompson, led by Jim Bazin. As earlier, the patrol led them out to sea. However, it was not one flying boat that they found but four (these being described as seaplanes in the squadron ORB), three in formation with another behind. Jim Bazin in Gladiator AF-N, leading the formation, was to describe these aircraft as Heinkel He 115s in his logbook. The threesome set about attacking the German formation but with no visible results. The 'no visible results' comes from the squadron ORB, although Jim Bazin was to note in his logbook, 'Four He 115s, one shot down'. The section returned to Acklington at 3.10 p.m. after seeing the German formation make good its escape, with the use of some helpful cloud cover. On their return, it was found that Bobby Pumphrey had set another new squadron 'first': he discovered two bullet holes through the fabric of his Gladiator's main plane.

The squadron's euphoria came to an end on Sunday 29 October. At around 10 a.m., F/O Alan Glover's Gladiator, K7997, crashed into the ground at Swarland Dene, some 5 miles to the west of Acklington. The squadron ORB states that the accident took place during formation flying, but it does not state how many other aircraft were in the formation, nor does it name any other pilot. Alan Glover had been a popular member of the squadron for over two years and he was cremated at West Road Crematorium, Newcastle upon Tyne, on Wednesday 1 November. Three days later his ashes were interred at Frodsham, Cheshire, with full military honours. An RAF guard from RAF Speke was to provide the military honours.[7]

In the early part of November, rumours began to circulate that a move to France may be imminent. These rumours were reinforced on 10 November when a civil Ensign flew into Acklington. Orders arrived in the evening that the squadron had to make ready to depart. Only one posting was uppermost in the squadron's mind: France. The fighter squadrons of the Advanced Air Striking Force had been in France since mid-September. However, three days later, the rumours stated that there was bad weather, putting an end to all flying. Yet, top of the posting list was still France, and so it proved to be.

Notes

1. Harry Welford, *The Unrelenting Years. 1916–1946*. Newton, 1997.
2. 607 Squadron ORB.
3. Francis Blackadder's correspondence with the family of Peter Dixon.

4. W.H.R. Whitty's personal correspondence with the author. Whitty also stated that he was flying Gladiator 'L' on the day. However, the logbook of Dudley Craig states that he was flying Gladiator 'L'.
5. The 607 Squadron ORB states that the rescue ship was a trawler that picked up the German crew 50–60 miles from the Northumberland coast. The intelligence report by Hilmar Grimm clearly states that they were picked up by the Destroyer HMS *Juno*.
6. RAF interrogation report of Hilmar Grimm, 22 October 1939. A 'history' of 607 Squadron, by the *Sunderland Echo*, appeared in 1971. The issue of 28 September 1971 states that the German pilot remarked, 'To be shot down by a bloody barrister in a bloody bi-plane is more than I can bloody well bear!' Judging by Fwb Grabbet's medical condition at the time, as well as his reticence to pass on any information, this statement has to be taken with a hefty dose of salt. In fact, this story was fictional, devised by British Intelligence. They noted in their report that pilot Grabbet merely stated that he was on a 'joy ride'. In the Air Ministry Weekly Intelligence Summary, 30 November 1939 issue, they released the concocted story for propaganda purposes.
7. Alan Glover's Gladiator, K7997, spun into the ground at Swarland Dene some 5 miles west of Acklington. His brother, Sub Lieutenant Alaxander John Glover, was also killed early in the war when he was aboard HMS *Gracie Fields*, which was sunk off Dunkirk on 29 May 1940.

CHAPTER FOUR

FRANCE: A BATTLE TOO FAR

It was the arrival of a civil Ensign aircraft on 10 November 1939 that first began the rumours of an imminent move. This was closely followed by orders received in the evening that the squadron should make itself ready for a move overseas. The following day did nothing to quell the rumours – due to bad weather; there was no flying and no further orders either. Although the weather was little better the day afterwards, it did allow flying, and two further Ensigns as well as a DH 86 flew into Acklington – proof, if any more was needed, that the squadron would soon be on the move. The following day was to heighten the rumours when three DH 86s and a Fokker transport flew into Acklington. The only official confirmation of a move came with the order that the squadron was to proceed to Croydon. Could this precipitate a move to France? After all, it was the obvious move, with the Advanced Air Striking Force (AASF) having been based there since September.

The aircraft were duly loaded and made ready in double-quick time. The Fokker was used for equipment only, while the DH 86 that had arrived on the 12th was available for personnel only. Adjutant George White was to travel in one of the Ensigns while James Vick was to travel in another. The whole squadron, having packed and made ready, had departed form Acklington by 2.15 p.m. Sticking to the coastal route, they made the point of flying over their home town of Sunderland, making a last farewell for who knows how long. The Gladiators then flew on to Digby, making a fuel stop there before moving on to Croydon, where they arrived at 5.20 p.m. While the move had gone smoothly enough for the fighters, there had been some small drama for the transports. Erroneous orders had been passed on to the civil aircraft; this resulted in them arriving at Heston unannounced. All of the 607 Squadron personnel aboard these aircraft were obliged to carry on their journey by specially drafted buses that eventually deposited them at Croydon at 9.15 p.m. The DH 86, along with the Fokker, leaving Acklington later than the other civil aircraft, could only make it as far as York and Digby respectively.

The following morning, the errant civil aircraft flew at first light, the DH 86 and the Fokker also making Croydon. Once again the weather was against the formation and it was not until 15 November that the formation departed for their eventual destination – Merville, France. While at Croydon, 607 Squadron had acquainted itself with 615 Squadron, another Auxiliary Air Force squadron. 615 Squadron was to join with 607

Squadron for the journey to France. At 11.30 a.m., the combined formation began its move from Croydon to Merville. Some forty-five aircraft in all took the route – from Croydon, via Shoreham and Le Treport, to Merville – with the Gladiators arriving at Merville airfield at 1.00 p.m. The whole trip had been fault free and Dudley Craig, flying Gladiator 'L', was to write of the trip, 'Good trip over'.[1]

The trip over may have gone well, although Merville airfield was not in its best condition. Weeks of relentless rain had caused much of the airfield to become waterlogged. The prevailing weather over the next few weeks was set to make Merville worse. The aircraft were immediately dispersed around the airfield perimeter. All routine maintenance was to be carried out at the dispersal point, with most of the work carried out in the open. The only shelter available was for the stores and equipment, and even this was made up of only a couple of Nissen huts. A further collection of tents provided much-needed shelter for the ground crews.

On arrival, the officers found that they had been billeted in the town. For the airmen there was only meagre comfort, as they were billeted in a large grain silo. This resided on the banks of the canal to the east of the town's railway station. All was not to be doom and gloom, however. Officers were wined, dined and entertained by their French counterparts. In early December, Francis Blackadder, Harry Radcliffe and Peter Dixon dined with a French unit, after which they attended a concert given by leading variety stars from Paris.[2] At the other end of the scale, Robert Walker, a mechanic on the squadron, remembers that a local French family regularly invited him and other airmen to their house for meals, washed down with wine. The same family provided them with much seasonal cheer during the Christmas period.[3]

Of course, 607 Squadron was in France for a purpose; that purpose being to provide air defence. On arrival at Merville the squadron had one day's rest, with patrols

A square near St Inglevert, used by pilots as billets. (Family of Dudley Craig)

St Inglevert, France. Three Gladiators are in the foreground. (Family of Dudley Craig)

beginning the next day. A section of 'B' Flight moved to St Inglevert to mount a patrol. However, no enemy was sighted and the section returned to Merville the following day. Dudley Craig states that this was a standing patrol between Cap Griz Nez and Dunkirk.[4] A false dawn came two days later when 'A' Flight sighted a He 111; however, the enemy spotted them in time and made good his escape without a shot being fired. This was to become the norm in what was described as the 'phoney war'; nothing, or very little, seen and no action. By the end of November, the weather began to get even worse, with the flying programme punctuated with the words: 'no flying today'. What had been a waterlogged surface at Merville rapidly gave way to a sea of mud over a foot deep in places.

There is always a brighter side, however, and this came in the form of a visit by the reigning monarch, King George VI. The King was to make an inspection of the AASF at Seclin, with representatives of each squadron based in France taking part. The representing of 607 Squadron fell to the commanding officer, Launce Smith, and 'B' Flight Commander, John Sample. The pair flew their Gladiators into Seclin on 5 December 1939 to take part in the rehearsals. The real thing was to take place the following day, and fourteen other ranks travelled by road transport to Seclin to play their part in the event.

The surface of Merville airfield had been getting steadily worse and much of the flying, apart from essential patrols, had been put off. The decision had been taken to move to Vitry, and an advance party set out on 11 December with the full squadron moving there by 13 December. Long-term squadron member James Vick was posted at this time to take up duties with 609 Squadron. His place as Flight Commander of 'A' Flight was taken over by Joe Kayll. The Gladiators were also becoming a bit tired and were flown to other airfields for their major maintenance. Dudley Craig reports that he flew Gladiator 'L' to

Douai for an engine change on 9 December.[5] Milne Irving made the flight a few days later on 15 December. Arriving there, Irving's Gladiator had overshot the runway and ended up in a dugout, damaging the Gladiator's propeller.

The weather was once again to take a turn for the worse. Where mud had been the bane of 607 Squadron's life at Merville, continuous frost with periods of snow made the surface of Vitry extremely hazardous. The squadron was to suffer a series of burst tyres and broken tail wheels, due mainly to the frozen potholes of the Vitry surface. Patrols were essentially of the 'Blighty' type, overflying the ships taking troops home on leave; these patrols were often carried out in a hazardous mixture of snow and fog. One of those going on leave at this time was Launce Smith, leaving John Sample in command of the squadron. During this period, due to the cold, the pilots wore their full Irvine flying suits. A contemporary photograph of the time shows John Sample in his full flying gear. For the ground crews, the harsh winter was to prove particularly severe, with maintenance being carried out mainly in the open air. Neither was there any comfort when they retired. Fires had to be kept well stoked all night in an attempt to gain them some heat. Most of the ground crew, if not all, were to sleep fully clothed to combat the cold. The persisting severe frosts meant that frozen aircraft engines were a normal, everyday occurrence. Robert Walker remembers that the engine oil was drained every night and heated every morning before being returned to the aircraft engine, in order to fly in a pre-dawn flight. Still the engines were to freeze on occasion. Robert Walker was to remember that Jim Bazin, whose aircraft had suffered in the frost, took a blow-lamp to his Gladiator's reluctant engine, causing many of the ground crew to retreat to a safer distance.[6]

Francis Blackadder was to report that Harry Radcliffe, on the return leg of a cross-country flight from Amiens on 2 January 1940, appeared to get lost and was forced to make a landing in a field some 5 miles south of Lille and approaching the Belgian border.

St Inglevert in the snow, January 1940. (607 (County of Durham) Squadron Association)

'B' Flight Commander Flt Lt John Sample in full flying gear. (Family of John Sample)

Pilot group. From left to right: Peter Parrott, -?-, Peter Dixon, Bobby Pumphrey, Francis Blackadder and Will Gore, with Launce Smith standing in the doorway. (Family of Dudley Craig)

A French Airforce Curtiss Hawk, St Inglevert. (Family of John Sample)

The Gladiator was undamaged and Joe Kayll was sent to retrieve it; he had no difficulty flying it out. Harry Radcliffe, on the other hand, was seen being 'interviewed' by Launce Smith, drawing the comment from Tony Forster: 'Look at Harry – he's got his best "bulls-hit" face on!'

Conditions were not to be much of an improvement at Vitry. The continual heavy frost intermixed with heavy snow showers made the airfield hazardous at best, with a spate of burst tyres and broken tail wheel, and fittings thrown in for good measure. The pilots and ground crew still managed to get the aircraft into the air, ensuring that the patrols were kept up. There were also co-operation flights to be flown in company with Lysanders. Three Gladiators of 'B' Flight took part in these co-operation flights, on 5 January 1940, but were grounded later in the day due to the usual broken tail wheel fittings. Neither was the accommodation an improvement at Vitry. The airmen were billeted in farms, with a number of senior NCOs at least being billeted in houses. A number of visitors were also to arrive during this period, giving the squadron some moral support. Captain H.H. Balfour, Under Secretary for Air, visited along with Air Marshal W.S. Douglas MC, DFC, the pair arriving on New Year's Day. Eight days later, on 9 January, Winston Churchill, first Lord of the Admiralty, arrived at Vitry in company with Air Commodore Capel. Patrols mounted during this period were flown mainly from St Inglevert, where 607 Squadron shared the airfield with various types of aircraft of the French Air force. While the squadron aircraft flew from one airfield to the other, the ground crew was transported by road transport.

While 607 Squadron aircraft were kept busy with patrols, the Luftwaffe was active as well. Mainly these were of the reconnaissance type of flight carried out at high altitude. Normally, by the time aircraft were scrambled in an attempt to encounter the high-flying aircraft, they had disappeared back to their base complete with their photographs. However, they were caught on occasion. On 13 January 1940, Red Section, comprising Peter Dixon and Bobby Pumphrey, led by Francis Blackadder, had such an experience. Blackadder noticed a white 'cloud', followed by two others, and broke away to investigate. In the climb he was passed by two Curtis fighters of the French Air Force making a dive for home. These were followed by a Do 215 which Blackadder witnessed crash near Calais Marc Airfield. The following day, Launce Smith telephoned the C/O of Calais Marc and arranged a visit to view the downed Do 215. Plinston, Blackadder, Bazin, Hawkes, Pumphrey, Dixon, Whitty and Stewart were among those that piled into the Hillman van en route to Calais Marc. All were surprised that the Do 215 seemed so small and was totally unarmed.

During this period, the main enemy was still to be the weather, the winter period of 1939–40 being one of the worst on record. Just to add a little misery to the men of 607 Squadron, all leave was cancelled on 29 January due to bad weather, and was not to commence again until 4 February. However, the weather failed to stop a new arrival on the squadron. Peter Parrott arrived on the squadron on 29 February, having been transferred from the fighter pool. In the meantime, Dudley Craig was having further trouble with his Gladiator. On take-off, the engine of the Gladiator cut out. Dudley Craig left the scene none the worse for his experience. Gladiator K6137; AF-Z, had arrived on 607 Squadron on 21 July 1939 from 72 Squadron. Now, with both its wings broken, the Gladiator was

Dornier Do 215 of 'A' Wekusta ob d1, brought down by French fighters near Calais. (Family of John Sample)

Charles E. Bowen at Wissant, January 1940. (607 (County of Durham) Squadron Association)

Photograph of Peter Parrott, in logbook of Francis Blackadder. (Family of Francis Blackadder)

confined to the scrapheap. A court of inquiry was subsequently held and Dudley Craig was found to be blameless.

The squadron received another visitor, on 24 February, when former Commanding Officer Runciman paid a visit to the squadron, staying overnight. The event was recorded with the usual photograph session, with some of the squadron pilots, Foster, Smith and Gore, being among the more obvious. On the weather front, next to hit the airfield was the thaw, and this was to bring a new set of problems. The airfields at both Vitry and St Inglevert became almost unusable, with Vitry being the hardest hit. Patrols were cut to an absolute minimum for operational purposes only. Traffic to and from the airfield was seriously curtailed and limited to lightweight traffic only.

Throughout the month of February the routine of the station was to remain the same. Patrols were mounted with the enemy rarely seen and, if they were, they used their altitude advantage to escape. Patrols were interspersed with air exercises in conjunc-

Maurice Milne Irving.
(Family of Francis Blackadder)

tion with various types of aircraft from differing squadrons, among them Lysanders, Blenheims and Battles. Group Captain Fullard, HQ, 14 Group, was to make a visit to the squadron on 9 March. Meanwhile one of the squadron originals, Flt Lt George C. White, was to make his departure from the squadron on 14 March. George White had been the squadron adjutant and Milne Irving now filled this role. Joe Kayll, another of the originals, was also posted at this time. However, he was only to move across the airfield, as his new squadron was 615 Squadron, and Joe Kayll was its new command-ing officer. The most significant change at this time came in the form of the Hawker Hurricane. Two of these aircraft were flown into Boos and earmarked for squadron service with 607 Squadron.

However, the squadron was still equipped with the Gladiator. Gloom was once more to settle on 607 Squadron, as on 24 March 1940, at around 11.40 a.m., a section of 'B' Flight consisting of Will Gore (Z), Nigel Graeme (B), Bobby Pumphrey (G) and Harry Radcliffe (F) took off from Vitry to carry out practice in No.1 attacks. Bobby Pumphrey was to act as target. Nigel Graeme, recently transferred from 'A' Flight, and Harry Radcliffe some-how came into contact. The two Gladiators, K8030 and K8000, spun out of control into the ground, killing both pilots. The bodies of both pilots were to lie in state at Vitry. The funeral took place on 26 March, and the cortege was escorted on foot at both ends, with the burials taking place at Douai Municipal Cemetery. Radcliffe was buried in Row 'L'; grave 11, while Graeme was buried alongside in grave 12.

Will Whitty. (Family of Dudley Craig)

That same evening, misfortune was to strike the squadron again although, on this occasion, the consequences were not as severe. Bill Whitty and Dudley Craig were scheduled to carry out night flying practice. However, during their flight, fog descended on the area around Vitry. The pair tried to locate Seclin and then Valencienne but failed, running short on fuel. Bill Whitty decided to vacate his aircraft and landed by parachute near Courcelles. Gladiator K7996 was written off after it crashed to earth. Dudley Craig 'felt' his way down, managing a forced landing in a ploughed field near Mons en Chausee, turning the Gladiator onto its back. Gladiator K7967, AF-L, had arrived on 607 Squadron from 87 Squadron, on 12 December 1938. It was eventually recovered but SOC at No.2 Air Service Park, on 28 March 1940. It was also during April that John Ryder Hawkes was to make his last flight as a fighter pilot; he failed an eye test during this period and was taken off flying. He remained with the squadron, however, as its intelligence officer. It was during this period, on 8 April, that John Sample, flying a 'split new' Master which had been ferried in by Bowen, distinguished himself by tipping the Master on its nose – the result of too much braking.

Rumours had been prevalent that the squadron was to be re-equipped with the Hawker Hurricane. Those rumours came to fruition on 12 April, when the whole squadron was moved from Vitry to Abbeville. While the squadron pilots made the move by air, taking off around 1 p.m., the ground crews were re-located by road transport, and all were reunited at Abbeville by early evening. Relief was to come to the ground crews in the form of Nissen huts, which replaced the tents and farm buildings vacated at Vitry. For the officers, the new mess (as well as the squadron HQ) was to be situated in a local chateau. The sergeants' mess was also moved up the scale, as the new one was situated in the lodge of the chateau. Pilots immediately got down to training in the Miles Master, flown to France for the purpose of converting pilots to the more modern fighter aircraft with a retractable undercarriage, something many had not experienced before. Peter Parrott was quoted as being one of the only pilots to have flown a Hurricane. He flew the first of the squadron aircraft on 8 April, having originally flown a Hurricane before his arrival on the squadron: 'I was the only pilot in the squadron who had flown a Hurricane and the most junior … '.[7] Most of the pilots were soon to gain experience on the basics of the Hurricane; they had no time to learn to fight with it. For Dudley Craig, the new experience of flying a Hurricane and leaving behind the First World War technology of the Gladiator came on 18 April, when he flew Hurricane 'M'.

The squadron was now equipped, mostly with the Hurricane, yet some Gladiators were to remain on the squadron. The morale of the squadron was described as very high. A return to Vitry was next on the cards and the move proceeded without a hitch, and all of the squadron was back at Vitry by 26 April. By now things were so quiet that a football match was played. Nine of the squadron were on the team representing 61 Wing when they played a team from 26 Squadron, the former winning 2–1. 607 Squadron also managed to win the cross-country running shield at a meeting at Gilsy. However, things were maybe a bit too quiet; as it turned out, it was the quiet before the storm. There was a very rude awakening for the AAFF in general, and 607 Squadron in particular. In the early hours of 10 May 1940, the German forces swept in force into Belgium and France: Blitzkrieg had begun.

The surprise with which the Blitzkrieg was mounted cannot be underestimated. 607 Squadron, in particular, had a number of pilots away from the squadron on leave in

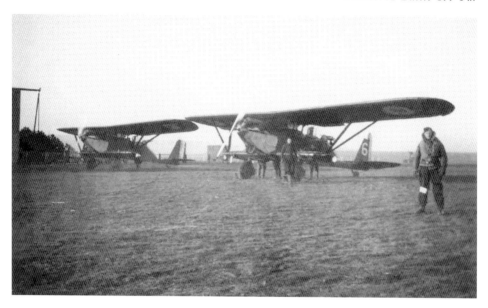

Two French Airforce Breguet BRE 270s (Family of John Sample)

A French aircraft (Family of John Sample)

Opposite page: A French Airforce Bloch MB 131. (Family of John Sample)

Crashed Miles Magister in France. (Family of John Sample)

French Airforce Breguet BRE 270. (Family of John Sample)

England. Dudley Craig was one – he had left France on 5 May 1940, and he recorded that he flew from Gilsy to Hendon in a DH 'Dragon Rapide' with F/O Heath as pilot. Presumably this was a ferry aircraft, as F/O Heath had no connections with 607 Squadron. While on leave in Somerset, Dudley Craig was recalled to 607 Squadron. Once more he was to make the trip, this time in reverse, from Hendon to Gilsy with F/O Heath, on this occasion making the trip in a DH Flamingo, a high-wing, twin-engine transport aircraft. During this period Launce Smith was also on leave, while the logbook of Francis Blackadder has a large, empty gap between 27 April–11 May. It is a reasonable assumption that this is indicative of a period of leave.

Most of the squadron members were still in their beds when the low-flying bombers of the Luftwaffe opened their attack on Vitry at around 4.15 a.m. The first 607 Squadron knew about it was the wailing of alert alarms at 4.15, followed by heavy gunfire as the pom pom guns opened fire against the enemy, with the accompaniment of the blast and shock of exploding bombs. Low-flying Me 109s also strafed the airfield, flying in low and fast from the west using the rising sun to their advantage. After the shock awakening, 607 Squadron were quick into action. Shortly after the initial attack, 607 Squadrons Hurricanes were in pursuit of the enemy. Peter Parrott in Hurricane P2574, AF-F, caught up with a He 111, pursuing it for some 15 miles without managing to close in on it: Firing at maximum range, he was forced to break off the attack after his ammunition was expended. Parrot was only allowed to claim the He 111 as 'possibly' damaged. Antonio Dini, in Hurricane P2572, AF-B, fared little better. Encountering a He 111 in the area of Conde, he expended most of his ammunition in the attack, resulting in smoke pouring from one of the engines. Antonio Dini was only allowed to record a claim of 'damaged'. To make matters somewhat worse, he was fired on by Allied anti-aircraft batteries, resulting in AF-A being slightly damaged.

Taking off a short time later, Jim Bazin was leading Monty Thompson and Sgt Ken Townsend when they encountered a He 111 in the area of Douai. Jim Bazin led the section into the attack and left the He 111 with a damaged engine. Monty Thompson was to follow up the attack, after which the He 111 began to go down. The pilot, Uffz Gerhard Kasten, was the only crew member to vacate the aircraft which eventually crashed near Cambrai. Flying Hurricane P2573, AF-A, Will Gore attacked a He 111 in the vicinity of Douai and saw smoke from both engines. He was to note that, 'When attacked, e/a turned into sun and remained so. Defensive fire from the "dustbin" put out of action in the third attack.' Will Whitty was also to make an attack on a He 111 of 7/KG1. Once again, only the pilot, Kurt Buchholz, was to make good his escape, with his aircraft coming down in the area of Hinacourt.

John Sample, in Hurricane P2615, was commanding the squadron in lieu of Launce Smith, and he led his section of John Humpherson and Charles Bowen towards another formation of He 111s of 11/KG1. Singling out a straggler, John Sample gave the bomber three bursts of gunfire but was forced to break off his attack when his windscreen became covered with oil from the enemy bomber. Both John Humpherson and Charles Bowen fired at the He 111 until forced to break off their attacks when their ammunition expired. The enemy aircraft was still flying when last seen. Tony Forster, who had taken off at around 11.30 a.m. in Hurricane P3448, AF-H, was with Yellow Section when they

Will Gore. (Family of Francis Blackadder)

encountered a formation of five He 111s of III/KG1 at 10,000ft in the area of Mons. After the attack, the He 111 was seen to crash. Tony Forster then turned his attention on another He 111 but could only claim it as 'damaged'.

No sooner were the aircraft back on the ground, rearmed and refuelled, than they were airborne once more, as a formation of He 111s had been located in the area of Albert. Noting that one bomber was straggling behind the rest, John Sample in Hurricane P2615 immediately initiated an attack. The He 111 was pouring smoke from its port engine when Sample began another attack. However, the other He 111s closed in and provided a heavy concentration of gunfire. The crossfire was to have its effect on Sample's Hurricane. Hit in the engine, it began pouring black smoke and oil, most of it covering the Hurricane's cockpit hood. The Hurricane was now crippled, and with visibility gone there was no chance of making a forced landing in safety. John Sample had no choice but to take to his parachute, and made a heavy but safe landing on the British side of the lines. However, he had badly sprained both ankles. Forced to wear carpet slippers, John Sample was grounded for the duration of the Battle of France.

The fighting was to continue at a furious pace. Sgt Ken Townsend was to make a claim for a He 111 as 'damaged' in the area of St Quentin. He jointly claimed another as 'damaged' with Peter Parrot, as they shot down another He 111 of 111/KG1 which was seen to crash near Cambrai. Monty Thompson carried out attacks on two He 111s, making claims for both as 'damaged'. Will Gore, in Hurricane P3448, AF-H, attacked a He 111 down the outside of the formation. With smoke pouring from one of its engines, Gore left the stricken bomber and carried out an attack on the formation leader with much the same result. In this action, Gore was allowed to make a claim for a third of a kill on two of the aircraft along with Tony Forster. Peter Parrot, in Hurricane P2536, AF-R, had joined forces with two French Morane 406s and had attacked a He 111, which they jointly reported as 'destroyed'. John Humpherson, who had taken off at around 2.50 p.m., was to claim a He 111 when, following an attack, both of its engines exploded.

In the final actions of the day, Arthur Eugene Le Breuilly and P/O C.R. Rowe, in Hurricane P2697, attacked a He 111. The enemy bomber, severely damaged, attempted a force-landing and was seen to crash into a house. P/O Rowe's Hurricane had been hit by return fire and was damaged. Red Section had taken off at 5.20 p.m. and had encountered seven He 111s of 6/KG27 in the area of Oudenaarde. Antonio Dini attacked the He 111 of Uffz Walter Zimmerman, and the enemy plane was seen to burst into flames. Bob Weatherill was also to claim a He 111 as a 'probable', while Dudley Trevor Jay in Hurricane P2571 made an unconfirmed claim for a He 111 as 'destroyed'. At 6.30 p.m., Yellow Section was in the air again and encountered a formation of around twenty-seven He 111s. Trevor Jay was to make a claim for two with Peter Parrot making a claim for one 'destroyed' and another 'damaged'. Peter Dixon was also to make a claim for one 'destroyed' but was hit by return fire and was forced to make a successful forced-landing. Antonio Dini, who had taken off at 8.40 p.m., was forced to break off an attack on a He 111 when his windscreen became covered in the enemy aircraft's oil. The first day of the battle had now drawn to a close but more was to follow next day.

The following day was slow to start. It was not until early afternoon that the action for 607 Squadron began. In three Hurricanes, Peter Parrott and Trevor Jay, with Will Gore leading, intercepted a He 111 between Douai and Derain. After carrying out their first attack, the enemy aircraft was seen to be trailing smoke but still flying. Trevor Jay then formated on the enemy aircraft to get a better look, but too late; he noticed that one of the gunners was still active. Trevor Jay became the target for a volley of gunfire and was wounded in the knee. He did, however, manage to get his Hurricane back to base. The He 111 was not so lucky. It was seen to shed at least one parachute before it dived earthward, where it crashed and exploded.

Shortly after, Francis Blackadder was leading Red and Blue Section near Brussels, when they observed a He 111. The He 111 was duly attacked and, after what was

607 Squadron pilots in France. From left to right: Peter Dixon, Will Gore, -?-, Bobby Pumphrey, Peter Parrott, Francis Blackadder and Launce Smith. (Family of Dudley Craig)

described as 'quite a battle', it was shot down and was seen to explode on an evacuated house.[8] While still circling the crash site, Peter Dixon noticed other enemy aircraft and alerted Francis Blackadder. For some reason, Francis Blackadder did not hear the call, and seeing Peter Dixon haring off he decided to follow. Formations of aircraft were identified but, before they could be attacked, they had joined another formation. Two of the He 111s had dropped behind the larger formation, Peter Dixon and Francis Blackadder attacked one each. However, the bombers were not alone. When the Me 109s began to make their presence felt, Blackadder and Dixon, both now short of fuel and ammunition, decided to beat a hasty retreat. Both the Hurricane pilots had over-stretched themselves; Blackadder ran out of fuel and was forced to land in a field. He later found some fuel and returned to base. Also out of fuel, Dixon made a landing in a field near Tirlemont, held by the Belgians, and went in search of fuel. On his return it was found that the Luftwaffe had made a raid in the area and his Hurricane was now a burnt-out wreck. Dixon returned to Vitry by road transport some twenty-four hours later. During this period, Jim Bazin had also carried out an attack on a He 111 and claimed it as 'destroyed'; Dudley Craig had claimed a Ju 87 as a possible.

On an early morning patrol the following day, Will Gore, in Hurricane P2572, AF-B, was leading a section consisting of Bob Weatherill and Gordon Stewart when they attacked a formation of He 111s. In the heated exchange the He 111s gave as good as they got, and consequently Will Gore's Hurricane was set ablaze. Managing to extricate him-

Peter Dixon, left, and Joe Kayll in France, 1939–40. Joe Kayll wears 607 Squadron flying overalls. (Family of Peter Dixon, via Simon Muggleton)

self, Will Gore suffered burn injuries and was admitted to a field hospital. Five days later, Will Gore was transferred to a hospital in England and his part in the Battle of France was over. For his actions, Will Gore was awarded the DFC. *The London Gazette* of 31 May 1940 carried the following citation:

> This officer, whilst leading his section in May, 1940, on a dawn patrol, intercepted a formation of three Heinkel He 111 aircraft. Due to his good leadership a determined attack was delivered with the result that all three enemy aircraft were shot down. F/O Gore's aircraft burst into flames immediately after the attack, but in spite of this he escaped successfully by parachute. This officer has for a long period shown great keenness and devotion to duty deserving of the greatest of praise.[9]

It is noticeable that a claim was made for all three He 111s as 'destroyed'. However, only one pilot, Gordon Stewart, was to return to Vitry to tell the tale. Will Gore was in hospital and Bob Weatherill was forced to land at Lille. Adding to the confusion, most of the paperwork was lost due to the squadron's hasty retreat from France. All three He 111s were known to have been destroyed. However, at least one He 111 from this formation was claimed by P/O John Cock of 87 Squadron.

A section from 615 Squadron was flown in to reinforce 607 Squadron. Francis Blackadder was in the air, at the head of a section consisting of Hurricanes from both 607 and 615 Squadrons, when they encountered a formation of Me 109s. The Me 109s were believed to be from 1/LG2, and a vicious dogfight ensued. In particular, Blackadder had difficulty shaking off his pursuers and arrived back at Vitry overdue, amid fears that he had been shot down. The Me 109s were to make claims for three aircraft shot down. However, only F/O Lewin Fredman, of 615 Squadron, was shot down. His Hurricane crashed near Liege.

Early on the 14th, Francis Blackadder was leading a section consisting of Peter Parrott and Tony Forster when, in the area of Louvain, they were bounced by Me 109s. Although they all managed to escape, Parrott's Hurricane had taken a few hits and, among other things, his radio was knocked out. Hasty repairs by the ground crew soon had it working again. Sgt Ken Townsend, P2616, was not so lucky. In the same area, he was shot down and taken prisoner, his Hurricane crashing near Ens-St-Servais. During a dig in 1992, a recovery group located and recovered the engine of P2616. Launce Smith, newly back from leave, was feeling anxious enough about Blackadder's section that he took off to search for them, arriving back soon after. Shortly after this, Smith was back in the air by 8.35 a.m. Leading a section consisting of Bob Weatherill and Tony Dini, they encountered a formation of Me 109s over Diest. In the ensuing battle both Smith and Dini made claims, with Smith's Hurricane showing signs of the battle.

During this period 607 Squadron were beginning to feel the strains of battle, as losses in both pilots and aircraft began to mount. To keep the squadron fully up to strength, pilots and aircraft were moved onto the squadron, most from England. Among the newly drafted pilots were P/Os R.D. Grassick, W.L. McKnight, P.S. Turner and Flt Lt J.L. Sullivan. Also, to relieve the Hurricanes, some Gladiators were moved from 615 Squadron to carry out local defence duties. These were flown by Staff Officers from the Air Component HQ, pilots and aircraft both being much needed. Casualties on the squadron were mounting daily. F/O G.I. Cuthbert, a new arrival on the squadron having been attached from 601 Squadron, was shot down and killed on the 14th. Cuthbert was believed to have been shot down by Me 109s of 4/JG2, the Richtofen Geschwader, his aircraft falling at Aische-en-Rafail. The son of Captain J.H. Cuthbert DSO and Kathleen Alice, Gerald Ivo Cuthbert was a local to the squadron and came from Corbridge in Northumberland; he was buried in Hotton War Cemetery. Lost the previous day, 13 May, was Monty Thompson, another local, from Newcastle upon Tyne. His Hurricane, P2620, was believed to have been bounced by Me 109s of 1/JG1 over the area of Tienen, with his Hurricane eventually coming down near Landen at around 5.15 a.m. Monty Thompson was originally buried in the Convent Cloister at Landen, his remains being reburied at Haverlee War Cemetery in early 1947.

F/O Arthur Eugene Le Breuilly was shot down on 14 May. Arthur Le Breuilly is thought to have joined 607 Squadron in April; however, the squadron ORB makes no mention of his arrival and, therefore, no mention of where he had been posted from. His memorial on the CWGC register states that he was, on his death, with 87 Squadron. That squadron was in France at the time and there may well be a tie. The author Peter Cornwell makes a claim that Arthur Le Breuilly was attacking Hs 123s in the area of Corroy-le-Chateau when he was attacked by Me 109s of 4/JG2 at around 10.55 a.m. He also claims that Arthur Le Breuilly was posted as 'missing'. The ORB of 607 Squadron states that Le Breuilly was 'killed', which makes it clear that someone must have known his fate. However, it is always possible that he was buried by locals, common practice during this time, in an effort to hide his remains from the German forces. In the heat of the ensuing conflict, those who buried him could have forgotten the burial place or have been killed themselves. Arthur Eugene Le Breuilly has no known grave and is remembered on the Runneymede Memorial, panel 9.

Although many of the patrols were straightforward scrambles to intercept the enemy, the larger number of the patrols was to escort bombers making an attempt to stop the advancing forces. Bill Whitty, speaking on escort duties, was to remark: 'We were ordered to escort Blenheims on rece flights but as they did these at naught feet we were of little help as AA was the main problem.'[10] On 15 May, six Hurricanes of 615 Squadron, under the command of Joe Kayll, flew into Vitry and joined forces with five Hurricanes of 607 Squadron's 'B' Flight. Launce Smith then led the combined force as it provided escort for Blenheims of numbers 15 and 40 Squadrons, the bombers making an attack on the bridges over the River Meuse. The Hurricanes were met with a force of Me 110s of Stab III/JG 52. A dogfight broke out as the Hurricanes fended off the attackers, Joe Kayll making a claim for two of the Me 110s. There were also Me 109s and it was one or more of these that attacked the Hurricane of Launce Smith. Hurricane P2870 fell away from the action over Dinant. Launce Smith was posted as missing and remains so today, having no known grave; he is remembered on the Runnymede Memorial. That the squadron was now hard pushed there is no doubt; on this day alone they flew some fourteen sorties. It may have been on this same day that Peter Dixon, pursuing an enemy bomber, ran out of oxygen. He continued the chase but was forced to admit he was: 'gasping for air', as he passed through 17,000ft. He was forced to land at high speed on his return to base, his Hurricane having sustained damage to its flaps. Peter Dixon admitted later: 'If I had done this in peacetime, I would have radioed for the fire engine and ambulance to be on readiness.'[11]

With their leader fallen, 607 Squadron gained a new commanding officer; Flt Lt George Morley Fidler was a Yorkshireman from Great Ayton. Detached from 14 Group, where he had been the armaments officer, to 607 Squadron on 11 January 1940, Fidler was now to lead the squadron into battle. The lack of experienced pilots is shown in the fact that Fidler had only a total of less than five flying hours in Hurricanes at this time. Peter Parrott, Peter Dixon, Stewart, Bob Weatherill and Bobby Pumphrey encountered five Dornier Do 17s on the 16th. Although all pilots reported seeing pieces flying off the bombers, the action was inconclusive and the Hurricanes, after using all their ammunition, were forced to break off the attack. However, in a separate attack, Dudley Craig reported that while flying Hurricane 'M' with 615 Squadron, they encountered a formation of Me 109s and he 'managed to floor one'.

Even by this date, defeat was beginning to look inevitable. The hordes of refugees were endlessly threading their way along the airfield perimeter. The ground crews were giving them any food that they had to spare, as the exodus moved towards the French coast. If the opposition of Me 109s was bad, then the fierce ground fire was even worse. Will Whitty, flying at between 13–14,000ft, had his Hurricane damaged when he was hit by ground fire; however, he managed to return to base where the damage was repaired. All of this added to the mounting pressure on the ground crews as they struggled to

607 Squadron pilots. From left to right: Will Whitty, Peter Parrott, Tony Forster, Launce Smith, Joe Kayll, Peter Dixon, -?-, -?-. (607 (County of Durham) Squadron Association)

make aircraft ready again as soon as possible – not the easiest of tasks. Spares were in high demand but not easily forthcoming. Aircraft too badly damaged were cannibalised for their parts. Others were forced to fly on with makeshift repairs that, in peacetime, would have seen them grounded.

Somewhat bizarre during this period, was the fact that, short of pilots though the squadrons were, some pilots were allowed home on leave. Peter Dixon awakened Peter Parrott and alerted him to that fact that there was an Ensign aircraft leaving for England and they could be on it. Already aboard the stripped-out Ensign were other pilots, including fellow squadron member Tony Forster. After a few short days, both Parrott and Dixon were ordered to Tangmere to join 145 Squadron. Back in France, however, the work still went on. A section of 'B' Flight encountered a formation of Dornier Do 17s near Cambrai. Bobby Pumphrey, Tony Dini and P/O J. Humphries all claimed victories. However, Blackadder, leading a section somewhat later, failed to make any contact at all. Dudley Craig, on an offensive patrol over Le Cateau, had a 'crack' at a Do 17 and saw it crash in flames. Shortly after he lined up a He 111 and saw it crash before he fired a shot. This may well have been the victim of another fighter unseen to Craig.

Both Blackadder and Gordon Stewart had their Hurricanes damaged on 18 May as a result of return fire from Do 17s. Blackadder was obliged to make a forced landing on his return to Vitry. Stewart also had to make a forced landing, returning to Vitry later. Bob Weatherill, carrying out a lone reconnaissance flight, appears to have been bounced by

Me 109s. Shot down, he is buried in Cambrai Communal Cemetery, his grave recorded as being: plot 2, row A, grave 13. His victor is credited as being Hptm Georg Mayer of 2/JG 51. Tony Dini encountered a formation of Do 17s over Cambrai. He was later to report that he broke up the formation, managing to cause damage on two, before forced to make a hasty retreat due to heavy return fire. Dini was not to be so lucky later in the day – when scrambling from base the squadron was badly bounced by marauding Me 109s. Dini's Hurricane suffered damage during this attack. During the afternoon, at around 4 p.m., while part of the squadron was in action over Arras, a formation of He 111s attacked the airfield at low-level. Aircraft at their dispersal points were damaged as well as boom tankers and fuel dumps.

The squadron was by now showing signs of being under strain and the airfield itself was coming under increasing attack. The word was passed to the squadron that they should make themselves ready to move with the minimum of kit. Along with 'B' Flight of 56 Squadron, 607 Squadron were withdrawn to Norrent–Fontes. However, there was not to be great deal of comfort at their new base. Will Whitty was to state: 'That night we moved out and many pilots slept in their planes at Norrent–Fontes.' Personnel were billeted in a deserted mining village nearby.

The squadron was back in action over Cambrai the following day. George Fidler was leading when they encountered Me 109s. In the ensuing battle, Fidler found himself pursued by a Me 109 that he had difficulty shaking off. Eventually, the Me 109 won the day as Fidler's Hurricane fell away. Sgt Leslie Rolls, behind Fidler when he was attacked, was himself put under attack. Managing to take evasive action, his pursuer overshot. He saw the other Me 109 attacking Fidler's Hurricane and fired on it. The Me 109 rolled over and dived to the ground. Flt Lt Fidler was at first thought to have been taken prisoner, as there were reports that his parachute had been seen. If this was the case then his parachute appears not to have deployed properly, as Fidler was killed. Flt Lt Fidler was buried in Bachy Communal Cemetery, the only serviceman buried there.

However, there is a French side to the story as well and this differs somewhat. A Hurricane was seen to fall away from the battle overhead and buried itself in a deep crater within a field known as 'Ferne Marchand' (Meadow of Wanehain-Bachy). The pilot, Flt Lt Fidler, also fell into a field, now a housing estate known as Allee des Comtes. The locals immediately turned up on the scene and found the pilot's body. First thing of notice was that Flt Lt Fidler was not wearing a parachute – presumably he had failed to take his parachute with him in the rush. When the pilot's body was moved, a depression was noticeable in the ground where he fell, even though the ground was described as dry and hard. The locals then proceeded to bury the body alongside where it fell so that the Germans would not be aware that the pilot had been killed. Sometime after the German occupation, the body of Flt Lt Fidler was removed from its burial place and reburied in the First World War soldiers' part of Bachy Communal Cemetery. As an honour to the fallen pilot, a local French Resistance group was named, S/Ldr Fidler.[12] The victor over Flt Lt Fidler may well have been a pilot of 1(J)/LG2; pilots of that unit were to make three claims for Hurricanes shot down in that area. It was at this time that the squadron personnel were warned to abandon all their kit and take only the bare essentials and depart in the direction of Le Havre.

However, the squadron pilots were still fighting on. While on patrol Bill Whitty and Jim Bazin came across a Ju 88. Approaching head-on they opened fire. Once passed, they slipped in behind and gave chase, and a running battle commenced with the pilot of the Ju 88 making every use of the available cloud cover. However, as often in air combat, although the Ju 88 was hit, the attack had to broken off inconclusively when the ammunition of the Hurricanes was exhausted. P/O J.S. Humphries also recorded that he made a similar attack on a Ju 88, with a similar outcome, and the Ju 88 may have been the same one that was attacked by Whitty and Bazin. Six of 607 Squadron's Hurricanes had been in action with a flight from 17 Squadron. Due to the situation on the ground, all of these aircraft returned to Hawkinge. The Hurricane of Whitty, damaged earlier by ground fire and suffering damage around the rear struts, was noticed on inspection to have had its struts clamped temporarily. Whitty had been advised that, when landing, to '… land with your tail up'. The repair, temporary or not, reflects the state of the aircraft that were flown in combat under pressure.

The following day the remains of 607 Squadron, some six Hurricanes, joined forces with 615 Squadron. Led by Joe Kayll, 615 Squadron's commanding officer, they were detailed to attack the German advance towards Arras, along the Cambrai road. Attacking in single file, all the aircraft came under heavy ground fire. Kayll's Hurricane suffered damage, as did the Hurricane of P/O Dick Demetriadi, who had to make a forced landing but made good his escape.[13] Bobby Pumphrey was not to be so fortunate. With his Hurricane badly hit, Pumphrey had to make a low-level parachute jump. Surviving his heavy landing, Pumphrey was taken prisoner by the Germans and was to spend the rest of the war behind the wire. For 607 Squadron, it was to be many weeks before they learned the fate of their fallen comrade.

For 607 Squadron, the Battle of France was now well and truly over. The remnants of the squadron were forced to make their own way home as best they could – for most this meant go any way that you can. Dudley Craig was to make the trip from Merville to Hendon as a backseat passenger in a Douglas flown by an unnamed Belgian pilot. That same evening, a Sabina aircraft departed with evacuees, and among these was Wing Commander Boret and his staff. Flying as escort to the Sabina aircraft were nine Hurricanes of 615 Squadron and four of 607 Squadron, repeating a ghostly reverse enactment of their flight to France in November. Dave Blomley, Ken Newton and P/O Courtney flew three of the Hurricanes, which on arrival in England were immediately scrapped. Blomley counted at least eighty-seven bullet holes in the aircraft, one of them having only three of its engine bearers left. For Vick Barnes, now with 504 Squadron, the passage had to be made by ship, if he could find one. This he did at the port of Boulogne. However, it was at the cost of his kit, which had to be heaved into the harbour. For the ground crews the journey was a nightmare as they moved from one port to the next looking for transport. For some the journey stretched along the French coast as far as Cherbourg. The road to France, filled with hope and anticipation only a few months before, now bore the bitter pill of defeat, as the British forces returned from the rout: the Battle of France was now over.

Notes

1. Logbook of Dudley Craig.
2. Correspondence from Francis Blackadder to Major J.H. Dixon, brother of Peter Dixon.
3. Personal conversation with Robert Walker.
4. Logbook of Dudley Craig.
5. Logbook of Dudley Craig.
6. Personal conversation with Robert Walker.
7. From the obituary of Wing Commander Peter Lawrence Parrott.
8. Correspondence from Francis Blackadder to Major J.H. Dixon.
9. *The London Gazette*.
10. Sqdn Ldr W.H.R. Whitty, quoted in Cull. B., Lander, B., and Weiss, H., *Twelve Days in May*, p.141.
11. Major J.H. Dixon, courtesy of the Dixon family.
12. Information from Bernard Brisset.
13. Richard Stephen Demetriadi, son of Sir Stephen KBE and Lady Demetriadi, was drafted in from 601 Squadron. He returned to that squadron on 21 May but was killed in action on 11 August 1940. He is buried in Cayeux-Sur-Mer Communal Cemetery, plot 1, grave 7. Wynn, in *Men of the Battle Of Britain*, neglects to mention Demetriadi's involvement in the Battle of France. His father was later to donate Ditchling Beacon to the National Trust in memory of his son.

CHAPTER FIVE

BRITAIN: DEFENCE OF THE REALM

France was now put behind them. The air fighting had been hard, not to mention the conditions under which the ground crews found themselves working and living. In the six short months, 607 Squadron had paid heavily in losses to both men and equipment. However, the British forces, now back in Britain, had to prepare themselves for what appeared to be a much harder fight to come. This was to be the defence of their homeland against what was now an all-conquering enemy force. With the benefit of hindsight, it is easy to view that little strip of water, the English Channel, as very wide. However, Britain was still reeling under the shock of defeat and that little strip of water looked increasingly narrow indeed. Although most at the time viewed the threat of invasion as very real indeed, the main object of the coming battle was aerial supremacy – the Battle of Britain. One nation's young men faced the young men of another nation. The battlefield was the flawless blue; the prize was the freedom to dominate the air space, a fundamental advantage in warfare. The battle itself has been much hyped over the years. For some, it won the war, for others it merely gave a breathing space before Britain attempted to get back into northern Europe once more. Various writers have narrowed the battle down until it has almost become the Battle of Kent with London thrown in. However, it was, as its title states, the Battle of Britain. The Luftwaffe was capable of roaming freely into every area of Britain and using it as a target. It involved every person in the British Isles, and was a defence of the realm.

The remains of 607 Squadron began to reform at Croydon from 22 May, with stragglers still turning up by 31 May 1940. From this date, new squadron members began to arrive, as well as 'old hands' who were returning. One of the latter was Harry Welford. Harry had been on the point of being sent to France when defeat overcame the British forces. Now he moved from 6 Operational Training Unit (OTU), to 607 Squadron, joining them from 18 June. Also arriving on the squadron this day were P/Os John Edward Sulman and Patrick Joseph Thomas (Paddy) Stephenson,[1] both RAF reservists from 3 Flying Training School (FTS). 'Paddy' Stephenson, of Irish birth, had been with Lloyds of London in pre-war days and would appear to have fitted into the mould of the Auxiliary Air Force quite well. One of the 'originals' to make a welcome return was Jim Vick, fresh from the Tangmere control room, and he was to take command of the squadron.

Francis Blackadder was to lament that, after the hectic period in France, Croydon was a fairly quiet place. He was also to record that 'A' Flight only comprised of two originals: himself and Milne Irving. Irving, who had fought like a Gladiator in the true sense of the word, had put up some sterling defence and was 'living an adventurous life' around the airfields of France. Although he had failed to shoot anything down, he had given many a fright, including himself. Over on 'B' Flight, only Dudley Craig, Will Whitty, Jim Bazin and Charles Bowen remained.

One pilot who was to leave the squadron at this time was Toni Dini. Although Dini had been on 607 Squadron only a short while he had earned his spurs in the fighting during the French campaign. Antonio Simmons Dini was born on 17 January 1918, the son of Pietro Antonio and Minnie Florence Dini of Christchurch, Canterbury, New Zealand. Toni Dini showed an early interest in all things mechanical and was educated at Christchurch Technical College, studying engineering. He was a keen sportsman and was a member of the rugby fifteen during 1935–36, as well as being a senior athletics champion. It was while at the College that Dini got his first taste of flying, when he flew with the College Aircraft Squadron. Dini left college with his University Entrance Certificate and Engineers Preliminary Certificate. On leaving college, Dini began work as a junior mechanic with the Christchurch Post Office and Telegraph Department.

In 1937, Dini successfully applied for a short service commission with the RAF. On his acceptance, Toni Dini sailed from New Zealand in December of 1937. In March 1938, Dini was commissioned with the rank of APO and the following month began his flying training at 3 FTS, Shillingford. On completion of his flying training, in October 1938, Dini was posted a Naval Co-Operation School for flying duties, while in May of the following year he was transferred to 750 Squadron of the Fleet Air Arm, flying Blackburn Sharks and Hawker Ospreys from Yeovilton, the squadron having only formed that same month.

Some four months later, Dini returned to the RAF when he was posted to 66 Squadron, only the second RAF squadron to be equipped with the Spitfire. However, Dini's stay with 66 Squadron was not to be long and he was seconded to Padgate on administrative duties. He was then transferred to 610 Squadron for a short period before being posted to France in April 1940, where he took up duties with 607 Squadron.

Dini was regularly in action during his stay in France and he remained on 607 Squadron until its return to England. However, when the squadron was reunited at Croydon, Dini was one of the pilots posted away. He was next posted to 605 Squadron, based at Hawkinge. However, Dini was not destined to stay long with 605 Squadron – he was killed in a flying accident on 31 May 1940, shortly before the squadron moved north to Drem. P/O Antonio Simmons Dini was twenty-two years old and is buried in Hawkinge Cemetery, plot O, row 1, grave 3.

At the end of May, heavy fighting was still going on in France, with the main limelight focused around the Channel port of Dunkirk. The squadrons flew daily patrols from their bases in the south to cover the evacuation of Dunkirk. One of these squadrons was 145 Squadron, flying from Tangmere. Peter Dixon had flown around ten sorties when, on 1 June, he was shot down over Dunkirk. Possibly trapped in his burning cockpit, Dixon eventually got free but his parachute was seen to be burning as he fell. He descended heavily into the water but was rescued. He was treated on the Mole above Dunkirk for his wounds and burns. Two days later, he was put aboard a ship for transportation home. The ship was bombed in Dunkirk and Dixon was killed in the attack. He is buried in Dunkirk Town Cemetery, plot 2, row 13, grave 16. With one of the few 'originals' gone 607 Squadron felt his loss keenly.

607 Squadron was soon moved back to their traditional home of RAF Usworth. Among the 'originals' making a return to the squadron was James Vick. Vick had left the squadron in France to join 609 Squadron. A traffic accident prevented Vick ever reaching 609 Squadron and he was returned to 607 Squadron as its commanding officer. Another 'original' to make a welcome return was Will Gore. Gore was to arrive on 607 Squadron on 22 June. Gore had just returned from some leave after leaving Torquay Hospital, where he had been treated for burns following his action in France. Wynn's *Men of the Battle of Britain* categorically states that Will Gore moved to 54 Squadron on 6 August, making a return to 607 Squadron in early September. However, there is no evidence for this. The squadron ORB makes no mention of Will Gore's coming and going between 54 and 607 Squadrons. 607 Squadron were on detachment to Catterick during early August, the same period as 54 Squadron were based there. Somewhere along the line, 54 Squadron, Will Gore and Catterick have been connected, drawing a wrong conclusion. It was during this time that 607 Squadron learned that some of its pilots had been decorated for their actions in the French campaign. Francis Blackadder was to receive the DSO, and Will Gore and John Sample were to receive the DFC. John Sample had now left 607 Squadron and, retaining the rank of Flight Lieutenant, joined 504 Squadron at Wick as its commanding officer. June was also to be a month of rest and recuperation. The squadron, still classed as non-operational, slowly began to claw its way back to strength with a mixture of old and new hands.

A number of new pilots were to join the squadron during this period. Among the sergeant pilots were W.G. Cunnington, who arrived from 7 Bombing and Gunnery School (Band GS) at Newton Down; G.A. Hewett, J. Lansdell and R.T. Glover, who all arrived from South Cerney. P/O Stuart B. Parnall also made a welcome return on 24 June. Stuart Parnall had formerly been with 607 Squadron in 1939 before moving to 7 Flying Training School (FTS) at Peterborough to finish his training. A spell with 263 Squadron at Drem was to follow before returning to 607 Squadron. To facilitate the night flying training programme, the squadron rotated its flights to Prestwick, the rotations being carried out throughout July. Ex-commanding officer Air Commodore Runciman AFC paid a welcome visit on 21 June, managing to stay over until the next day. New arrival Flt Lt F.M.F. Plinston arrived on 20 July from 6 OTU, remaining with the squadron until 2 August when he returned once more to 6 OTU.

Although the air fighting in France was behind them and the squadron was officially 'resting', the training of new pilots had to go on. The new faces had turned up, mainly from the flying schools where they had been taught to fly the Hurricane. Now on a fighter squadron, they had been taught how to use the fighter to its advantage. The training of pilots could be fraught with as much danger as any aerial conflict and this was brought home to the squadron on Wednesday 26 June. Sgt Richard Thomas Glover had only joined 607 Squadron six days previously and was still classed as a 'new boy'. His

Hurricane, N2706, AF-F, encountered some sort of problem in the area over Sedgefield, County Durham. The Hurricane crashed from altitude into Neasless Wood, ½ a mile to the south of Sedgefield, killing its pilot. Sgt Richard Thomas Glover was the son of Norman and Irene Gladys Glover of Brailsford, Derbyshire. The twenty-two-year-old pilot was buried in Thornaby on Tees cemetery in plot O, row N, grave 3. Perhaps it was due to his short stay on the squadron that his name, and this accident, is missing from the squadron ORB.

On 28 July 1940, 'B' Flight flew down to Catterick where it took up position as an operational Flight, carrying out air gunnery tests against targets in the sea. The ground crew of some nineteen men and one senior NCO were to make their usual leisurely way by road transport. After a few days, 'B' Flight returned, its place being taken by 'A' Flight, who flew down to Catterick on 3 August. F/O Tony (Bunny) Forster was another 'old hand', who made a welcome return on 15 August, after spending a period with 151 Squadron.

However, 15 August 1940 was to become a memorable day for 607 Squadron. On this day, as part of an all-out front against the air defences of Britain, Luftflotte Five, from its base in Norway, was to make a concentrated attack on the north-east of England. The primary target for this attack was the fairly obscure bomber airfield of Dishforth, Yorkshire. A diversionary feint carried out by Heinkel He 115 seaplanes gave way to the main force of some sixty He 111s of KG 26, escorted by some twenty-one Me 110s of 1/ZG 76. 72 Squadron from Acklington met the attack initially, then later a flight of 605 and 79 Squadrons joined in. The attacking force had drifted slightly off course and had been mauled prior to reaching the Tyne estuary. By this time, it was thought an attack on Newcastle or the Tyne may be about to commence.

It was at this time that 607 Squadron were brought to readiness well in advance, maybe too much in advance. Harry Welford stated that they '… sat around the "Flights" for half an hour'.[2] The squadron was then scrambled into action but suffered from the fact that no-one seemed to know where the enemy was. The squadron was first vectored one way, then the other, as they were sent on a tour of most of County Durham. Returning once more to the area of Usworth, having been informed it was to be put under attack, they were then sent to the mouth of the Tyne and, at this time, were patrolling at 20,000ft. At last the shout 'Tally Ho' came from Francis Blackadder, as the enemy was spotted some 5,000ft below over Whitley Bay, north of the Tyne. Francis Blackadder was in command of the squadron as James Vick, much to his annoyance, was on leave that day. The majority of the fighter escort had by now gone, and 607 Squadron got stuck into the bombers. Joining them this time was 41 Squadron from Catterick. Harry Welford was to single out a He 111 an initiate an attack: 'I chased a Heinkel and filled the poor devil with lead until first one and then the other engine stopped and I had the sadistic satisfaction of seeing the plane go into the sea.'[3] This was to be Harry Welford's first 'kill'. On his way back to Usworth to celebrate, he flew his Hurricane at rooftop height down Newcastle's Northumberland Street. He first contemplated flying under the famous Tyne Bridges but thought better of it!

As 607 Squadron pursued the He 111s down the Durham coastline, Francis Blackadder was to make a claim for a He 111 destroyed off Seaham Harbour. This may have been on his combat report but it is at variance with his logbook, in which he credits himself with 'Two uncertain and a third of a kill certain'. Francis Blackadder was also to state that he attacked a Do 17, but there were no Do 17s on this raid. The Me 110 had twin rudders, as did the Do 17, and Francis Blackadder may have attacked one of the Me 110s of the fighter escort. Dudley Craig, flying Hurricane 'L', was to make a claim for two He 111s, pursuing the He 111 for some 60 miles out to sea before oil pressure trouble forced him to turn for home. Sgt Burnell-Phillips was to make a claim for a further two He 111s destroyed. The enigmatic Peter Burnell-Phillips had originally joined the RAF as an acting pilot officer and passed through the RAF College of Cranwell. He was forced to resign his commission in February 1939, when he was found guilty of some illegal low flying. He was to re-muster in the RAFVR as a Sergeant and was awarded the DFM on 1 November 1940. He was commissioned once more in November 1940 and was killed in a flying accident at Haddington, Midlothian, on 9 February 1941.[4]

Although another linked attack was to take place further south in Yorkshire, 607 Squadron had fought its battle of the north-east and defended their homeland over their hometown. On this day the Luftwaffe had been decisively beaten and this was the only time that was to happen in the whole of the Battle of Britain. Many had made claims for 'kill' and many were rejected in the cold light of day. 607 Squadron's ORB states that the score for the squadron was: six He 111s and two Do 17s destroyed; five He 111s and one Do 17 as probables; four He 111s and one Do 17 damaged, with no losses to 607 Squadron. Francis Blackadder records the score in his logbook as, 'Ten certain, eight damaged some of them badly'. The claims are a little on the high side and what are shown as Do 17s should have been Me 110s. The similarities come about because both Do 17 and Me 110s had twin fins, and the addition of a large fuel tank under the nose of the Me 110s gave it a Do 17 look. Among those who took part on those days were, from Red Section, Blackadder, Welford and Cunningham; from Yellow Section, Burnell-Philips; from Blue Section, Bazin, Parnall and Hewett; from Green Section, Craig Whitty and Maughan.

The squadron was to lose another of its pilots on 1 September 1940 due to an accident. Peter Clarkson Weeks (91228) appears to have been on 607 Squadron's strength on paper only, although Francis Blackadder stated that he was on the strength of 'B' Flight. Weeks is recorded as being on the squadron from 24 August 1939, when he was referred to as Mr Weeks with no flying training at all. He was reported as still being on the squadron on 20 October, when it was noted he still had no flying training. He was then posted to No.11 E & RFTS at Perth before moving on to 15 Service Flying Training School (SFTS) at Brize Norton. It was during this period that Weeks was gazetted as an acting pilot officer with 607 Squadron, on 27 March, even though 607 Squadron were at this time in France. Weeks returned to the strength of 607 Squadron once more on 31 August 1940, having been attached to 5 OTU, but was immediately passed on to the Usworth Station Flight with effect from the following day, 1 September. The same day, flying Hurricane N2586, Weeks was seriously injured when the Hurricane crashed near Usworth airfield. Weeks appears not to have done much flying after this date. He was gazetted on 21 June 1942 as a flying officer on probation (emergency) while attached to the RAF Administration and Special Duties Branch. He was again gazetted, on

Hawker Hurricane number P2874, AF-F, was the personal Hurricane of Francis Blackadder. A note on the rear of the photo states that this was taken after the attack on the north-east on 15 August 1940, and that patches cover bullet holes from an He 111. (Family of Francis Blackadder)

15 December 1944, as having his commission relinquished on account of ill health, and retaining the rank of Flight Lieutenant.

With the end of the events of 15 August, 607 Squadron returned to normality. The squadron was once more to send its Flights in rotation to Catterick. John Humpherson DFC was to make a return to the squadron on 23 August. John Ryder Hawkes, still on the squadron as the intelligence officer, was promoted to the rank of Flight Lieutenant on 3 September, with *The London Gazette* entry not appearing until 24 April 1941. Only a short while later, John Ryder Hawkes resigned his commission with the RAF, on 22 July 1941. 'A' Flight made its return to Usworth from Catterick on 31 August, and was met with rumours that the squadron was to depart south. In reality this was to happen on 8 September.[5] 607 Squadron departed Usworth and flew south to Tangmere, by way of Bicester. 607 Squadron were to take over from a battle-weary 43 Squadron; what must 607 Squadron have thought of the 'Fighting Cocks'? Harry Welford was to leave his thoughts: 'We arrived at a completely blitzed aerodrome and were greeted by the remains of 43 Squadron, some with crutches, others with their arms in slings and yet another with his head swathed in bandages, having had his face torn by an exploding cannon shell.'[6] Obviously, judging by the state of 43 Squadron's walking wounded, there had been plenty of action. The pilots were soon to find out that Tangmere was kept fairly busy. No sooner had they landed and refuelled than they were back in the air, scrambled into action to patrol Shoreham at 15,000ft. However, as often happened, there was nothing to be seen and the squadron returned to Tangmere.

The big raid of the following day was directed against south London and its suburbs. With the bombers in the air and making progress towards their targets, radio messages were intercepted warning formation leaders to turn back if '… the defences were too strong, or if the protection was too weak'.[7] However, new into the battle area, 607 Squadron were to prove to be a little 'green'. Attacking the bomber force over Mayfield, 607 Squadron were to be badly bounced by Me 109s of the ever-watchful fighter escort.

The bomber force consisted of a mixed bomber formation of around sixty to seventy Ju 88s and Do 17s flying in a northerly direction at around 15,000ft. James Vick, at the head of the squadron, ordered Blue Section to attack the bombers from underneath with the Hurricanes still in a climb, while Green Section was to protect the rear. The fighter escort had been seen above, and Red and Yellow Sections climbed into the attack already at a disadvantage. The Me 109s, flying at around 19,000ft, on both sides and the rear of the bombers, saw them coming and pounced, making 607 Squadron pay dearly for their mistake. Among those who fell were Stuart Parnall, who's Hurricane P3574 crashed at Lime Trees Farm, Goudhurst; P/O J.P. Lenahan's Hurricane, P3117, fell at Mount Ephraim, Cranbrook; and George Drake's Hurricane; P2728, was posted as missing. Burnell-Phillips was slightly wounded when his Hurricane, P2912, made a forced-landing near Knockholt. Sgt Richard A. Spyer was wounded when P2680 made a forced landing on Stilstead Farm, East Peckham.

Richard Alfred Spyer was the son of Richard Alfred and Violet Edith Spyer of Worcester Park, Surrey. Richard Spyer had joined the RAFVR prior to the outbreak of

Hawker Hurricane AF–U, thought to be at Usworth, 1940. This aircraft was often flown by Dudley Craig and Will Whitty. (The late Sqdn Ldr W.H.R. Whitty)

Hawker Hurricane, P2728, the aircraft flown by P/O George Drake when he was killed on 9 September 1940.

the Second World War, and after flying training at 10 FTS, Tern Hill, he had been posted to 111 Squadron at North Weald. For further Hurricane experience, Richard Spyer was posted to 607 Squadron. There is no further mention of him in the squadron ORB; however, he is shown in a photograph at Tangmere with Francis Blackadder and Milne Irving, so he may have returned to the squadron after his injury. Richard Spyer was killed with 261 Squadron on 22 March 1941 in the Battle of Malta. He is remembered on the Malta Memorial, panel 2, column 1. He was twenty-three years old.

A further Hurricane, it and its pilot unidentified, was stated as probably another victim. In its first encounter with the Luftwaffe in the south, 607 Squadron had paid a heavy price for their inexperience. Almost half the squadron's aircraft had been lost in one encounter. The comrades of the fallen were forced to admit: 'We bit back the tears and sorrow.'[8] George Drake, posted as missing on 9 September 1940, was to remain so until May 1972, when a wreck recovery group unearthed the remains of his Hurricane. The remains of George Drake found their last resting place on 22 November 1972 in Brookwood Military Cemetery, where they were interred with full military honours. Although he was a South African, the Commonwealth War Graves Commission has him listed on their website as being of the UK.

On 11 September, John Humpherson rejoined the squadron along with P/O Franciszek Surma, who was posted from 151 Squadron. Franciszek Surma, known as Franek, was one of the more charismatic Poles on 607 Squadron. He was born on 1 July 1916 in Galcowice, Rybnik, in Polish Silesia, the son of a peasant farming family. On 1 September 1936, Surma joined the Polish Air Force. In May of the following year, Surma was attached to the Infantry where he was to remain until July, when he made a return to the Air Force and was posted to the 2nd Regiment with the rank of Staff Sergeant. From September

1939, Surma was with 121 Eskadra Mysliwska, a fighter squadron attached to the Krakow Army, heavily involved in the defence of Poland. In the early morning of 1 September 1939, 121 Fighter Squadron of 111/2 Fighter Wing of the Krakow Army Air Arm was involved with elements of the Luftwaffe over Balice Airfield. As a result of the action, the CO of Krakow Fighter Wing was killed.

When Poland eventually fell to the advancing German forces, Surma departed Poland via Romania and Syria and travelled on to France, and from there he eventually made his way to England, arriving in early 1940. Once there, Surma was commissioned as a P/O in the RAF, on 24 January. Surma was initially posted to 15 EFTS for further training before he was posted on to 6 OTU at Sutton Bridge on 18 July 1940. It was at Sutton Bridge that Surma was converted onto the Hawker Hurricane. After completion of his flying training, Surma was posted to his first fighter squadron, 151 Squadron, based at North Weald. While flying with 151 Squadron, Surma was to make a claim for his first 'kill': an He 111 on 30 August, the squadron at that time flying from RAF Stapleford. When 151 Squadron was withdrawn from the Battle of Britain for a rest, Surma was posted to 607 Squadron, arriving there on 11 September. Surma was to claim a Me 109 as 'destroyed' over St Catherine's Point, Isle of Wight, on 11 September 1940.

Another of the Poles to be posted to the squadron was Boleslaw A. Wlasnowolski, posted two days later from 32 Squadron. While on patrol on 13 September over the area of Beachy Head, Francis Blackadder came across a Ju 88 at 13,000ft. Attacking the bomber with a short burst, Blackadder could only watch as the Ju 88 escaped into some convenient cloud cover. Only a short while later, however, he attacked another Ju 88 in a head-on attack. On this occasion, his gunfire found its mark. Smoke trailed from one of the engines of the Ju 88 and its undercarriage dropped down. Once more, however, the Ju 88 was to make use of cloud cover. After a short look around, Blackadder discovered yet another Ju 88. As with the others, it was to make good its escape using cloud cover. Blackadder had to be content with the claim of one enemy plane as 'damaged'. However, to further add to his discomfort, Blackadder's Hurricane ran short of fuel and he was forced to make a landing at Shoreham before returning to Tangmere.

14 September saw 607 Squadron in action twice over the coast between Poole Harbour and the Needles. Yellow and Red Sections, the latter consisting of Milne Irving

Groundcrew thought to be at Tangmere, 1940. On the left is F/Sgt Barret-Atkin, and on the right is Sgt Fort. Blackadder's 'F' stands at the rear. (Family of Francis Blackadder)

Wilfred P. Olesen, Jim Vick and Will Gore, Tangmere, 1940. (Family of Francis Blackadder)

and Sgt Cunnington led by Francis Blackadder, attacked a Ju 88 until it was seen to enter cloud trailing white and black smoke. The group decided 607 Squadron should claim this aircraft as a 'kill'. The second sortie turned out not to be so lucky. Once more attacking Ju 88s from the rear, Francis Blackadder reported that he attacked one. Although Sgt Cunnington, Will Gore and Tony Forster all had a go at it, the Ju 88 made good its escape. Other elements of 607 Squadron were hampered by the fighter escort, a mixture of Me 109s and 110s diving down on them. The combat eventually ended as inconclusive.

15 September 1940 was to go down in history as Battle of Britain Day; the day recognised as the height of the Battle of Britain. 607 Squadron was involved in the afternoon attacks which crossed the coast and moved in a north-westerly direction. Airborne at 2.45 p.m., 607 Squadron encountered the enemy at around 3.15 p.m. in the area above Appledore. Two groups of around forty to fifty Do 17s were spotted as they merged into one group at around 15,000ft, the attacking force having apparently already dropped their bomb loads. The squadron was wheeled round to the front and initiated a head-on attack down the left-hand side.[9] As the attack got under way, Horst Schulz, a crewman aboard a Do 17 of KG 3, was transfixed with horror – a Hurricane was bearing down on the nose of his aircraft at an alarming speed. The Hurricane shot over the top of the Do 17, barely missing it, and collided with another to the rear. This was the Hurricane V6688 belonging to Paddy Stephenson. After the collision, Paddy Stephenson abandoned his Hurricane over Cranbrook and landed safely, although slightly injured with a broken ankle. The Do 17 of 5/KG3 crashed into Cambwell Wood near Goudhurst where it exploded, killing its crew of Oblt Becker-Ross, Obfw. Bruckner and Fw. Hansen, with Fw. Brinkmann missing, presumed killed.

607 Squadron pilots in Schubin PoW camp. From left to right: Joe Kayll, Bobby Pumphrey, Dudley Craig and Alan Beales. (Family of Dudley Craig)

Although this is not a book on the Battle of Britain, the exploits of Patrick Joseph Thomas Stephenson, known as 'Paddy', on the afternoon of 15 September 1940, deserve a mention. Earlier that day a Do 17 of 1/KG 76, en route for London's docklands, was attacked by around eight fighters, the coup de grâce being delivered by a Hurricane of 504 Squadron when it collided with the Do 17 over London. The Hurricane was, of course, that of Ray Holmes, a sergeant pilot on 504 Squadron. His combat report, written shortly after the event, notes that he carried out no less than four attacks on the Do 17 and, while carrying out his third attack, the crew vacated the Do 17. Ray Holmes' report then states, 'On my fourth attack from the port beam, a jar shook my starboard wing as I passed over the E/A and I went into an uncontrollable spin'. The report clearly points to the act being an accident rather than a deliberate ramming of the Do 17. The ramming theory had been passed down into the myth of Battle of Britain literature as fact, which it was not. The Do 17 was eventually credited to at least six pilots, with the exception of Sqdn Ldr John Sample, CO of 504 Squadron and Holmes' boss, who is missed from most (if not all) of the reports on this event.

In the afternoon, formations of Do 17s were flying over the area of Appledore when 607 Squadron attacked them by means of a head-on attack. During this manoeuvre, a dangerous one at the best of times, the Hurricane of 'Paddy' Stephenson collided with a Do 17 of 5/KG 3, the end result being that the Do 17 crashed into Cambwell Wood

Sqdn Ldr John Sample at Exeter, as commanding officer with 504 Squadron.

504 Squadron, Exeter: John Sample is fourth from the left, centre row. Vick Barnes is second on the right, centre row. (Family of John Sample)

near Goudhurst. The Hurricane of 'Paddy' Stephenson also crashed, its pilot taking to his parachute slightly injured. It may have been an accident caused by the head-on attack rather than a deliberate ramming of an enemy bomber. However, pilots or any writers of aviation history commemorating the events of 1940 never enhanced the story of 'Paddy' Stephenson's collision. Over the years Ray Holmes' story changed from, '... a jar that shook my starboard wing', to one of the accepted versions such as, 'I went right on in and hit the Dornier'. This was the way Stephen Bungay phrased it in his book, and perhaps this can be seen as the story of two Dornier 17s 'downed' in similar circumstances. One, a straightforward, no-nonsense attack, while the other is deeply shrouded in the myth of the Battle of Britain and enhanced over the years by a sensationalist media.

At around 5.45 p.m. a further encounter with the Luftwaffe took place over Poole Harbour and the Needles. The squadron initially vectored towards Southampton before small groups of Do 17s were spotted. On this occasion the squadron was to carry out an attack from the rear. Some 3,000ft above the bombers were the fighter escort, who continually dived down on the Hurricanes in an attempt to keep them at bay. Even so, 607 Squadron were to claim two Do 17s as destroyed when they were seen to crash into the sea.

On the afternoon of 17 September, Jim Bazin was at the head of Blue and Green Sections. 'A' Flight was already airborne, having been scrambled into action to make up a fighting unit, and Blue and Green sections joined up with 213 Squadron. 607 Squadron took up the rear, acting as rear guard as the aircraft patrolled at 17,000ft. The weather was adverse to bomber missions on this day, the result being that large numbers of fighters were on patrol instead. Only a small number of bombers were used as bait in order to lure the fighters of RAF Fighter Command into the air. As 607 Squadron's Hurricanes carried out their patrol, the Me 109s, flying at high altitude, dropped on the two squadrons almost simultaneously over Gravesend. In the ensuing attack, two Hurricanes fell away from the formation. Hurricane P3933 was to crash to earth at the 'Bell', Beltring, killing its pilot, Sgt John Lansdell. Hurricane P3929 was hit in the bottom of its engine and its pilot, Harry Welford, was to make a forced landing on Tuesnoad Farm, Bethersden. Welford was slightly wounded, having hit his head against the gun sight as a result of the landing. It would appear that 602 Squadron were at some times flying with 607 Squadron. 602 Squadron's commanding officer, Sandy Johnstone, was to report of the event, 'later in company with 607 Squadron and, while climbing through 21,000 feet, we were jumped by some 109s coming out of the sun. Indeed the first we knew of their presence was when Jimmy Vick's two weavers keeled over with smoke belching from their engines after which the 109s shot off at such a rate that we had no earthly chance of catching up with them.'[10] Hauptmann Eduard Neumann, Grp Kdr, 1/JG 27, was to make a claim for both Hurricanes.

Sgt John Lansdell had joined 607 Squadron at RAF Usworth on 19 June 1940. John Lansdell, a Fellow of the Royal Aeronautical Society, had a first-class Honours Diploma in Aeronautical Engineering, and was the son of William Albert and Ellen Sarah Landsell of Great Yarmouth. John Landsell had joined the RAFVR prior to the outbreak of war, and had been called up in September 1939. He arrived on 607 Squadron from 3 Service Flying Training School, South Cerney. John Lansdell was twenty-three years old when he was killed, and is buried at Hempnall (St Margaret) Churchyard.

If the last few days had been hectic, the following were to prove to be the quiet follow-ing the storm. Although the Battle of Britain raged on (indeed, this was the acknowledged height of the battle), 607 Squadron played little part. It was around this time a photograph was taken at Tangmere, showing mostly ground crew, Francis Blackadder and Milne Irving: two of the ever-diminishing number of 607 Squadron originals. Two new arrivals to boost the squadron numbers were pilot officers Derek Gould and Norman Heywood, who arrived at Tangmere on 22 September, both pilots having completed continuation training with 32 Squadron then based at RAF Acklington, Northumberland. 32 Squadron, as with most other squadrons, rotated from the south for a 'rest' in the north, doubled as a training squadron, providing combat training for pilots mostly from OTU. Back in action again by 24 September, the efforts of 607 Squadron were to prove fruitless. Dudley Craig said of his patrol over London: 'Nothing seen all day.'[11] Will Gore, leading the squadron, was to have little more luck. On patrol over Southampton and the Isle of Wight, his attention was drawn to some enemy aircraft by exploding anti-aircraft fire. However, they were too far away and once again there was no interception. The replacement pilots still continued to arrive at Tangmere, with pilot officers William W. McConnell arriving from 32 Squadron and Hamilton C. Upton arriving from 43 Squadron on 25 September. Milne Irving was on patrol that morning but had the same result as Will Gore – having spotted a He 111 it was too far away to intercept.

On the afternoon of 26 September, the Luftwaffe, after forming over the coast of Brittany, made a concentrated attack against Southampton. The main object of the attack was the Supermarine works, builder of the Spitfire, at Woolston.[12] Half the squadron was already in the air, and these were later joined by the others, the whole squadron being led by Francis Blackadder as they vectored towards Southampton. Heavy anti-aircraft bursts denoted the presence of enemy aircraft, and Blackadder formed the squadron into sections line astern for the attack. With the initial attack over, the squadron broke up and carried out individual attacks. It was probably during this encounter that Peter Burnell-Phillips, having exhausted his ammunition, made repeated mock attacks on a Do 17, attacking it so vigorously that it was to crash into the sea. 607 Squadron were to claim the destruction of one Do 17 and a Me 109, with a Ju 88 claimed as 'damaged'. However, the raid against Woolston had only been opposed by anti-aircraft fire; the defending fighters did not arrive on the scene until the bomb-ing was over. The Luftwaffe raid had achieved what it set out to do. The Itchen works was destroyed, as was the Woolston works.[13] Charles E. Bowen was to be the squadron's only casualty on this day when his Hurricane, P5205, was shot down. He managed to vacate his Hurricane successfully and landed by parachute in Calbourne. Later Francis Blackadder was to make an attack on a He 111 with two bursts of two seconds each. Blackadder was to watch the He 111 go through a series of stalls before pitching into the sea off the Needles.

Scotsman Alec M.W. Scott joined 607 Squadron on 27 September, after serving a short period with 3 Squadron at Wick, Scotland. More action was to come to the squadron the following day, and from 28 September, the Luftwaffe tactics were to change. The mass bomber formations had not achieved the required results and the fighter escorts had been much hampered by being forced to stay with the bombers, which used more fuel trying to keep formation, therefore losing time over England. The bomber formations were of smaller numbers and, more often than not, faster bombers mainly of the Ju 88 and Me 110 variety. However, the number of fighters in the escorts went up dramatically and formations of over 200 fighters were normal, the fighter formations being stepped up from the bombers as high as 30,000ft. These fighters in the high escort had the advantage of being able to swiftly drop down on any unsuspecting fighters, carry out a swift attack, be gone and rejoin their comrades before the defending fighters had time to realize what had happened.

The afternoon of 28 September saw 607 Squadron making its fourth sortie of the day, patrolling a line between Beachy Head, Selsey Bill and Bembridge at around 12,000ft. Will Gore was at the head of the squadron as it patrolled back and fourth for over an hour. There has been suggestion that the controllers were not up to par on this day and some controllers were being trained.[14] Eventually the controllers stated that there many enemy aircraft at 20,000ft to the east of Selsey Bill. Will Gore ordered 'A' Flight to follow him up and investigate: 'B' Flight, for some reason, could not keep up and fell back, eventually patrolling Portsmouth instead. With 'A' Flight still in the climb, the Me 109s of the high escort dropped on 607 Squadron and hit them hard. Most of the Hurricanes were to suffer some sort of damage in the attack and could count themselves lucky to escape. Two Hurricanes fell away and crashed into the sea. These were P3108 of Will Gore and R4189 of Milne Irving. Two other Hurricanes were to carry out an attack on a Do 17, identified as a Do 215, at 5,000ft south of Selsey Bill. However, these were driven off by Me 109s before they could get close enough to deliver any damage. The bodies of Will Gore and Milne Irving were never found, and the squadron must have mourned their loss deeply as both had been on the squadron so long. The names of Will Gore and Milne Irving are remembered on the Runneymead Memorial. Among the Luftwaffe aircraft taking part that day were JG 2, JG 26 and ZG 2. Later in the day, Francis Blackadder was to lead a section as they made a fruitless search for Milne Irving and Will Gore.

The squadron was back in action on 30 September. In the vicinity of Chesil Beach and Portland, twenty Me 110s were encountered at around 4.45 p.m. In sections line astern 607 Squadron carried out a head on attack in an attempt to break up the formation. The Me 110s broke up and moved out to sea where they formed defensive circles as they awaited the bombers to escort home. Some thirty to forty Do 17s and Ju 88s were next sighted, and 607 Squadron, now broken up, carried out individual attacks on these without result. During this encounter, Jim Bazin was to make a claim for one Ju 88 'destroyed' and another as 'probable'. Jim Bazin never mentions details of encounters in his logbook, merely stating what his flight was for. In this case, 'operational' is all that he entered.

The following mornings 607 Squadron were sent off to patrol Swanage at 20,000ft. Control informed them that enemy formations were moving in from the south-east. However, when the enemy was spotted there were three formations, each of around twenty aircraft and they were approaching on a course from west-north-west at 18,000ft. The bombers were thought to be in the bottom group and this was the group 607 Squadron attacked. However, what were thought to be bombers turned out to be Me

110s who turned to meet that attack of 607 Squadron, and a running dogfight broke out which drifted to the Isle of Wight. Once again 607 Squadron were to suffer at the hands of the Luftwaffe. In the ensuing dogfight, two Hurricanes fell away, victims of the fighter escort. Hurricane P2900 with Charles E. Bowen aboard was classed as 'missing, presumed dead'. Hurricane V6686 with Sgt Norman Bramby fell near the Isle of Wight, killing its pilot. Mason was to state that both Hurricanes were shot down by Me 110s near Swanage.[15] Among the Luftwaffe fighter escort that day were 1/ZG 26, 4/JG 26 and 1/JG 51.

New pilots were still arriving on the squadron to replace those that had gone. F/O Ivor B. Difford arrived on 2 October from 85 Squadron, based at Church Fenton. P/Os Gustaw Radwanski and Michael R. Ingle-Finch both arrived on 3 October from 151 Squadron. Gustaw Radwanski was born on 2 May 1913, and in his pre-war days was trained as a psychologist. With the collapse of Poland, Gustaw Radwanski made his way to England where he arrived in late 1939, and was commissioned into the RAF as a P/O in January 1940. Having completed his flying training, Gustaw Radwanski was posted to 79 Squadron and later to 151 Squadron. After only ten days Gustaw Radwanski was posted away from the squadron, on 13 October, and arrived on 56 Squadron the following day.

Gustaw Radwanski was later posted to 302 Squadron and then to 316 Squadron. It was while he was with the latter that he survived a mid-air collision with Sgt Musial, although the latter was killed, on 13 February 1942. Radwanski was to spend most of the rest of his RAF career on training duties and was released from the RAF with the rank of Flight Lieutenant in 1946. A photograph of Radwanski taken with Franek Surma at Tangmere survives to mark his passing with 607 Squadron. Further action for the squadron commenced on the afternoon of 4 October. Francis Blackadder, flying as Red 2, led the squadron when it was ordered to patrol the area over St Catherine's Point. Once airborne this was changed to Swanage at 20,000ft, with 607 Squadron taking up a patrol line between Swanage and the Needles. At around 2 p.m., Blackadder saw what appeared to him to be enemy aircraft some 3,000ft higher. Reporting this to Jim Bazin, he received no reply and, due to some radio quirk, Bazin never received the query from Blackadder. It was during this short period of hesitation that the Luftwaffe struck. Confirmation of an impending attack came from Green 1, P/O John Sulman, who warned that enemy aircraft were diving down on the rear of the squadron. The warning almost came too late, as the squadron was bounced. Luckily, the squadron managed to break in all directions and escaped any major damage. However, a number of the Hurricanes were hit and four had to make forced landings, with a further six suffering damage of various description. On their return to Tangmere, 607 Squadron counted itself lucky to have survived to live to fight another day.

F/O Derrick Gould moved away from the squadron on 5 October, joining 601 Squadron at Exeter. Almost no action came the squadron's way on 7 October. The squadron's Operation Record Book reports nothing seen. However, two of the squadron's Hurricanes managed to collide with each other at around 4 p.m. Hurricane L1728 collided with Hurricane P3860 over the area of Slindon. F/O Ivor Difford, only five days on the squadron, was trapped in the cockpit of L1728 when it crashed near Slindon, taking its pilot to his death. The South African pilot from Johannesburg was later buried in Tangmere (St Andrew) Churchyard, where his grave is in plot A, row 3, grave 483. Ivor Difford was the son of Captain Ivor Denis and Elfride Geraldine Difford of Johannesburg, Transvaal, South Africa. P/O Alec M.W. Scott, the Glaswegian former Brasenose College (Oxford) student, was luckier. He managed to take to his parachute, landing near Slindon, from where he returned to the squadron. Scott's Hurricane, P386, crashed onto Eartham Farm near Slindon.

It was now felt that 607 Squadron had done enough in the south. The squadron had been hard hit while at Tangmere, as well as having to train its new pilots, and was in need of a rest. A number of new pilots arrived on 9 October, eight of which were British and twelve were Poles. They all arrived from 5 Operational Training Unit or 615 Squadron, and all were in need of further training. The following day, 607 Squadron flew its final patrol along with 602 Squadron, over Swanage at 24,000ft. However, only friendly fighters were seen. On return to Tangmere, the whole squadron departed north to RAF Turnhouse, Edinburgh. For some there was a stop-off at Usworth, while Francis Blackadder reports that he stayed at Catterick for two days, following the squadron on 13 October. Jim Bazin also recorded that he made a stop at Catterick beFore going on to Usworth. The following day he proceeded from Usworth to Turnhouse. Once there, the CO, James Vick, bid his farewells to the squadron, as he was to take up his post as Wing Commander Training with 14 Group the following day. The new commanding officer was to be Sqdn Ldr A.W. Vincent, who was posted in from 8 Bombing and Gunnery School (B&GS).

For Jim Vick, his second departure from 607 Squadron was also to be his swansong as a fighter pilot. Will Whitty was to state that it was around this time that Jim Vick failed an eye test after which he passed on to Training Command Number 14 Group. Jim Vick was to remain in the RAF until early 1942, at which time he was released from RAF service and seconded to the civilian airline, Imperial Airways. He was to serve with that airline in the capacity of organisation and administration. Jim Vick was to remain with Imperial Airways for the rest of his career, serving in various places throughout the world. Squadron lists show that Jim Vick was with Cyprus Airways Ltd, based at Nicosia in the post-war years. Jim Vick died in 2002 aged ninety-four. The new commanding officer, Sqdn Ldr A.W. Vincent, was to remain with 607 Squadron until March 1941, when Dudley Craig returned to take command. Sqdn Ldr A.W. Vincent was then promoted to the rank of Wing Commander and posted to command 4 E.F.T.S in South Africa.

Franek Surma was posted away on 17 October and arrived on 46 Squadron the following day, moving on four days later to 257 Squadron at RAF North Weald. Franek Surma was to make a claim for a He 111 as a 'probable' on 28 October, while the next day he narrowly missed being shot down himself when Me 109s carried out a low-level attack on North Weald. In December, Franek Surma was posted to 242 Squadron, and in March of the following year sent to 308 (City of Krakow), claiming a share in a 'probable' destruction of a Ju 88.

Shortly after this, 308 Squadron were equipped with the Spitfire, with which Franek Surma claimed a further four kills as well as surviving an aircraft fire in Spitfire R6644. A few weeks later, 308 Squadron were to join the Polish Wing at RAF Northolt and carry out fighter sweeps across France. 8 November 1941 saw 308 Squadron taking part in a 'circus' to escort bombers that went tragically wrong. Due to the bright sunlight 308 Squadron turned in the wrong direction and turned up in a hostile area. Caught unawares, they were bounced by Me 109s and Surma went 'missing' during this action. Surma had been promoted to F/O on 1 March 1941 and was awarded the KW and Bar, on 10 September, followed by the award of the Virtuti Militari on 10 October 1941, the latter being presented by General Sikorski. Surma is remembered on the Polish Air Force Memorial at RAF Northolt. Pictorially, a few photographs of him survive, mainly dating from his days at Tangmere with 607 Squadron.

From this time the whole of 607 Squadron was to change, as more new pilots began to arrive for training and the longer serving pilots moved on, taking their experience to other units. P/O Alec Scott was to move to 249 Squadron while P/O McCormack was to depart to 257 Squadron and P/O Radenski to 56 Squadron. Long-term pilot Francis Blackadder was to depart on 24 October, temporarily at first. This move was confirmed when he was posted to Turnhouse (Ops) on 6 November. Will (Nits) Whitty was next to go when he was posted to 6 OTU Sutton Bridge as a flying instructor on 3 November. For Peter Burnell-Phillips there was the award of a DFM on 1 November 1940, the citation reading:

> One day In August, 1940, this airman displayed great skill when, by determined tactics, he forced a Dornier to crash into the sea although he had expended all his ammunition. On another occasion he destroyed a hostile aircraft after his own had been severely damaged and he had received a bullet wound in his foot. He has displayed exceptional skill and gallantry in his attacks against the enemy and has destroyed at least five aircraft.[16]

Still more of the long-term squadron members were to be on the move. Dudley Craig was posted to Turnhouse as a supernumerary (Ops) while Jim Bazin DFC was to be posted to RAF Catterick for operational duties. Tony Forster DFC was posted to Central Flying School (CFS), Upavon, for course number 17, a flying instructor's course. Joining him at Upavon was Harry Welford and Hamilton Upton while Flt Lt Cedric Stone DFC was posted onto the squadron from 254 Squadron, where he had been a Flight Commander. These movements took place on 15 December 1940. On the 20th of the month, John Humpherson was posted to the Aeroplane and Armament Experimental Establishment (A&AEE) at Boscombe Down for test pilot duties. John Humpherson was later to move on to 90 Squadron and was killed on 22 June 1941, flying a Boeing B-17 with that unit. The B-17 broke up mid-flight and crashed at Catterick Bridge. John Humpherson was buried in grave 93, Heslington (St Paul) Churchyard, Yorkshire. P/Os R.G. Lauder and John Storrie were the last two to leave 607 Squadron in 1940. P/O Lauder was posted to 96 Squadron and John Storrie was posted to 2 Central Flying School (CFS) at RAF Cranwell to take up a flying instructor's course.

Before moving on, there should be a few words on the activities, or lack of activities, of P/O R.G. Lauder. Robert George Lauder (78531) was gazetted as a P/O, RAFVR, on 17 April 1940. After his training he was posted to 263 Squadron, then flying Gladiators in Norway. While awaiting the movement of the ship, he was diverted to join 607 Squadron,

From left to right: Tony Foster, Orzechowski and John Lauder. (Family of Dudley Craig)

then based at Usworth. P/O Lauder arrived at Usworth, on 1 June 1940 to take up flying duties. Although he was to remain with the squadron until December 1940, there is no mention of him taking part in any operational flying. Considering this period lasted throughout the Battle of Britain and there was supposed to be a shortage of experienced pilots, this is odd. He is not named on any list or book as having taken part in the battle and the squadron ORB fails to mention that he is still there or anywhere else. Evidence that he was still on the squadron during this period lies in the logbook of Dudley Craig. Although not mentioned in any activities, he appears on four photographs of the period. He was also noted, by Francis Blackadder, as being on the strength of 'A' Flight during this period. His only further mention in the Squadron ORB is for 26 December 1940 – it records that on this day he left to take up flying duties with 96 Squadron at Cranage. What happened to P/O Lauder during his time with 607 Squadron remains a mystery. While at Cranage, P/O Lauder is known to have crashed while attempting a landing in Hurricane, V7130, on 11 January 1941, presumably with little or no injury. He again had a mishap in Hurricane P3833 while landing at Cranage on the night of 15–16 February. He was gazetted as a flying officer on 17 April 1941, and was later posted to 73 Squadron. It was while flying a Hurricane of this squadron, based at Sidi Hamaish, that he was shot down and killed. His body was never recovered and he is remembered on the Alamein Memorial, column 241.

With the end of 1940, 607 Squadron had passed through a memorable piece of British history. It had fought with distinction throughout the Battle of France as well as the Battle of Britain. More changes and challenges were to face the squadron through 1941. Once more the squadron was to move to Scotland; this time it was to be Macmerry,

East Lothian. With the influx of regular airmen the squadron had taken on the mantle of a more regular RAF Squadron, and in doing so had lost much of its territorial individuality with which it had been born. Many of its pilots were to go on to serve more distinguished careers. However, 607 Squadron, with its distinguished service record, was to remain bloodied after its battles, but unbowed.

Notes

1. The 607 Squadron ORB states that Stephenson arrived on 18 June 1940, yet Wynn, in *Men of the Battle of Britain*, states that he arrived on the squadron sometime in July.
2. Harry Welford, *The Unrelenting Years 1916–1946*, p.108.
3. Harry Welford, *The Unrelenting Years 1916–1946*, p.108.
4. The 607 Squadron ORB clearly states that Burnell-Phillips was the only pilot involved. Harry Welford, p.105, states that Burnell-Phillips took two Polish pilots with him adding, 'what a terrible waste'.
5. Both Welford, p.112, and the 607 Squadron ORB state that the squadron moved south on 8 September. Bungay, *The Most Dangerous Enemy*, p.313, states that 607 Squadron arrived at Tangmere on 1 September.
6. Welford, p.112.
7. Wood and Dempster, *The Narrow Margin*, p.350–351.
8. Welford, p.112.
9. The 607 Squadron ORB clearly states that the squadron attacked down the left-hand side. Bungay, p.327, states that 607 Squadron attacked down the right-hand side.
10. The 607 Squadron ORB states that this attack took place on 17 September, with no recorded assaults for the following day. AVM Sandy Johnstone CB, DFC, AE, states that this action took place on 18 September.
11. Logbook entry of Dudley Craig.
12. Jeffrey Quill, *Spitfire: A Test Pilot's Story*, p.184, states that Woolston was put out of action completely, as was the Itchen works. Production was moved to other districts.
13. Jeffrey Quill, p.184.
14. Sqdn Ldr W.H.R. Whitty stated that new controllers were being trained on this day. Personal correspondence with author.
15. Mason, *Battle Over Britain*, p.347.
16. *The London Gazette*, 1 November 1940 issue.

CHAPTER SIX

SOME MEN OF NOTE

Any squadron, whether RAF or AAF, is dependent on one vital ingredient without which no squadron can survive or function: the men. It is the men of a squadron that gives it its vital lifeblood, its personality, its structure, its sole and its very being. Also, there are some of its members who are better known than others. There are always some who seem to rise above all others, either by their actions or just their sheer personality. In this section I would like to give prominence to some of the men of 607 Squadron. That is not to say these men are better than their peers. For one reason or another they have been singled out as being different from the others. This may be as a result of their character or as a result of their achievements. They may have been thrust to the fore by means of a single achievement, or by the result of a number of achievements combined. Either way, they have left their own stamp on the squadron, their own little piece of individuality.

WALTER LESLIE RUNCIMAN

Walter Leslie Runciman, known as Leslie, was the first son of Walter Runciman MP (later Viscount Runciman of Doxford) and his wife Hilda, *née* Stephenson. Both parents were active in politics, with Walter Runciman being a Liberal MP in Asquith's government and Hilda Runciman being the MP for St Ives, Cornwall. The Runciman family origins lay in Scotland where Leslie's grandfather, also Walter, was born in Haddingtonshire, but in reality East Lothian. Walter ran away to sea at an early age and on his return worked mainly in shipping and its ancillaries. Eventually, Walter Runciman was to set up home in the Northumberland coastal village of Cresswell. In later life he was to form the shipping line the Moor Line, and became Baron Runciman in the process.

The life of an MP almost demands two addresses; in the case of Walter Runciman, these were to be London and Newcastle. Walter Leslie Runciman was born on 12 August 1900, in Newcastle upon Tyne. From his birth, Leslie Runciman had a lot to do to live up to his predecessors. Education began at Eton, his father's old school. Following on from Eaton, Runciman became a King's Scholar at Trinity College, Cambridge. Moving from Cambridge, Runciman began his career as a chartered accountant in the firm of Deloitte. This was to be seen as good grounding for any future career within the family shipping

business. It was during his time in London that Runciman met the woman who was to become his first wife. Rosamond Lehmann was a graduate of Girton College and was later to become a novelist of some repute. The next move for Runciman was northwards to Liverpool. There, he began his apprenticeship with the shipping company of Holt before moving further north to Newcastle upon Tyne.

The Runcimans began their new life in the north with a new home. Number 3 Sydenham Terrace, in the residential are of north Newcastle, the house having been a wedding present from Leslie's grandfather. Runciman was to work for the Moor Line, the shipping company owned by his grandfather, and he was to be directly answerable only to him. This was not to be an enviable task it seems, as grandfather Walter Runciman was known to one and all as the 'beast'.[1] During the General Strike of 1926, Leslie Runciman played his part by serving as a special constable. His wife, Rosamond, never really developed a liking for Newcastle, and in later years she was noted as even avoiding using the city's name. However, they socialised well and among their circle were notables such as the Ridley's of Blagdon. However, their time was divided between the north and the south of the country. With Rosamond as a novelist, the Runcimans balanced an uneasy alliance between the 'arty' set and the business empires of the north. On one side were the northern families of influence and power, while on the other were those such as Rosamond's sister, the actress Beatrix Lehmann, Lyton Strachey, as well as the artists Dora Carrington and Augustus John. However, the Runcimans were further cut off from the south when they moved to their new house, Annick Cottage near Hexham, Northumberland. It came as no surprise when, in 1928, the Runciman marriage collapsed.

It was also around this time that Runciman began his association with flying. Surprisingly, Rosamond's biographer makes no mention of this activity. Likewise, the 'Who's Who' of 1989, the year of Runciman's death, fails to mention this association and also fails to mention any association with 607 Squadron or the Auxiliary Air Force. However, it is known that Runciman was an accomplished pilot and had had some success in the King's Cup Air Races of this period. He also owned his own aviation company. A photograph taken in 1929 shows a Gypsy Moth that had landed in a field near Leyland, Devon. No explanation is offered as to why it landed but the pilot's name is given as Leslie Runciman. In all probability, the flying visit to Leyland was all part of a public relations exercise for his mother, Hilda Runciman, MP for St Ives. It was the following year that Runciman was appointed squadron leader and commanding officer of the newly forming 607 (County of Durham) Squadron.

In 1932, Leslie Runciman married his second wife, Katherine Schuyer, younger daughter of William Garrison and Clementine Schuyer of New York. There was one issue from the marriage: Walter Garrison Runciman, known as Garry. In later years he was to become a well-known sociologist and eventually succeeded his father as Viscount Runciman. On 12 March 1936, Runciman was awarded the AFC in recognition for the part he played in forming and building 607 (County of Durham) Squadron. With the beginning of the Second World War, Runciman was promoted to the rank of Wing Commander and transferred to the General List. He also relinquished command of 607 Squadron but kept his ties with the squadron as he took over as Honorary Air Commodore from the Marquess of Londonderry when the latter's tenure ended. In this role he managed to keep contact with 607 Squadron through some of its hardest battles in the Battle of France as well as the Battle of Britain.

Still retaining his civil business commitments during this time, Runciman remained deeply involved in the family shipping business of the Moor Line, Doxford Co. Ltd and the Anchor Line. He was also to retain a healthy interest in aviation, and civil aviation in particular, when, from 1938, he was on the boards of both Imperial Airways and British Airways, becoming an influential force in the eventual amalgamation of the two airlines, cumulating in BOAC. In 1947, he was to resign as part of a protest over the weak and negative attitude of the government towards the development of civil aviation. In 1949, on his father's death, he succeeded him as Viscount Runciman of Doxford. Runciman also managed to serve on the board of Lloyds Bank for some forty years.

As some of his last service in the RAF, Leslie Runciman served as Air Attaché in Tehran, Iran. For his services there, Runciman was awarded the OBE on 4 June 1946. With the end of the Second World War, Leslie Runciman returned full-time to his business concerns at the head of his shipping lines and aviation interests, also becoming deputy lieutenant of Northumberland in 1961. Runciman suffered a serious injury around 1986 and never fully recovered from the after-effects. On 1 September 1989 he died of an illness related to his injury of some three years before, and was cremated at Golders Green Crematorium. However, the RAF never forgot Leslie Runciman and honoured him with a memorial service at the RAF Church of St Clement Danes, London, on 19 November 1989.

WILLIAM HENRY NIGEL TURNER

William Henry Nigel Turner, eldest son of Captain Edward Algernon Turner and his wife, Edith May, née Cotgrave, was born on 6 January 1910, on the Island of Dominica, West Indies. Captain Turner was a master on the Royal Mail Line and the family originated from Somerset. It is thought that Captain Turner took his wife along on one of his trips, which is how his son came to be born in the West Indies. William Henry Nigel Turner was always known within the family as Nigel. In later years, however, especially those that were spent with 607 Squadron, Turner became known as Willy. For the sake of simplicity he will be referred to as Willy throughout this text.

Education for the young Willy Turner was by way of St Peter's School, Bristol, before moving on to Clifton College. With aviation still in its infancy during this period, and aeroplanes still looked upon as a novelty, they had the ability to draw crowds wherever they went. It was during this period that Turner was photographed sitting in an aeroplane. On this occasion it was an aeroplane of the Cornwall Aviation Company Ltd of St Austell, probably one of an increasing number of aviation companies that toured the country giving cheap rides. No doubt, Turner had paid his fee and was awaiting the coming flight, destined to be the first of many.

There was to be no doubt about Willy Turner's interest in aviation. When he left Clifton College there was only one place to go as far as Turner could see – the RAF. He also needed to justify his education, and to this end he applied to and was successful in entering RAF College Cranwell. Willy was to begin his studies at the RAF College in August 1929 and they were to last until 25 July 1931. After Cranwell came Turner's first posting to a squadron and this would appear to have been 40 Squadron. After its disband-ment at the end of the First World War, 40 Squadron had reformed by 1 April 1931, so was new when Turner joined it at Upper Heyford, Oxfordshire. Number 40 Squadron flew the Fairey Gordon in the light bomber role. Willy Turner was to remain with 40 Squadron until he was posted overseas in early 1933. His next posting took him to 45 Squadron, based at Helwan, Egypt. It was on 17 March 1933 that Turner recorded his first solo flight, in a Fairey IIIf, 9812.[1] This was a flight up to 1,000ft for circuits and landings. The precise Turner recorded that the flight took place at 11.00 a.m. His first 'away' flight was to Heliopolis in a Fairey III, 9162, the flight being made with F/O Tutnall. There then followed a series of high bombing practices from 6,000ft and low-level bombing runs as well as some photographic flights. Turner did his share of mail deliveries as well as a number of visits to other landing grounds. Among these were Khatatba, Armina and Aswan, thrown in with a few landing practices. The year 1935 saw King George V's Silver Jubilee and the RAF marked these, even in the outposts of Egypt. Turner flew Fairey III JR9827 in one such event – the Jubilee Formation Flypast over Cairo which took place on 6 May. In July 1935, Turner was to depart from 45 Squadron and return to the UK. On leaving the squadron he was assessed as above average as a pilot. He moved next to Uperavon where he was to embark on a flying instructor's course at the Central Flying School (CFS).

From the Central Flying School, Turner was posted to 6 Flying Training School (FTS) at Netheravon. His first flight at Netheravon, as a flying instructor, was made on 17 December 1935. On this day he flew Avro Tutor, K3391, with LAC Foster. In all, Turner was to make eight flights that day. Turner was to stay at 6 (FTS) until July 1936, his last flight being in K3388 with APO Thomas, the pair making a flight to Tangmere and back. Following a short leave, Willy Turner was posted to 9 Flying Training School (FTS). His first flight after arrival there was recorded as being on 27 July 1936 when he flew in K7311 on flying practice, although the type of aircraft was not recorded. On 18 August 1936, Turner flew Hawker Hart K6490 to Bircham Newton and back. His passenger on this occasion was APO Peter Brothers, later to fight in the Battle of Britain with 32 Squadron. Turner's last flight with 9 (FTS) came on 1 July 1937. On this day he flew Hawker Auadax, K7328, to Hullavington and Netheravon with A/C Bell in the back seat as ballast.

Turner was to take his skills as a flying instructor to 607 Squadron, based at Usworth, County Durham. He arrived there in July and records his first flight as being on 24 July 1937, when he flew Hawker Hart K6482. This was a routine training flight with trainee pilot Peter Dixon in the other seat. A number of photographs of Turner survive from this period, as he seemed to make himself available at all the social events as well as the annual summer camps. Turner was to remain with 607 Squadron until February 1939. His final two official flights took place on 17 December, firstly in Avro Tutor, K3407, when he flew with Mr Headlam on an air experience flight and later, in Hawker Hart, K6482, when he flew with P/O Harry Radcliffe on a routine training flight. However, with Christmas out of the way, Turner made a return to Usworth and made his last flight from Usworth as a 607 Squadron pilot. This was on 6 February 1939, when he flew Gloster Gladiator, K7782, on a twenty-minute flight that he recorded as 'air practice.'

Turner had been posted back to an operational squadron within Bomber Command. This was 51 Squadron based at Dishforth, Yorkshire, the squadron at that time flying the Armstrong Whitworth Whitley. The Whitley was the largest aircraft Turner had flown so far, and he was to be the commanding officer of 'B' Flight. Turner's first flight was to be on 9 February 1939, when he flew as second pilot in Whitley, K8978, with F/O Baskerville, the purpose of the flight being to allow Turner to convert onto the Whitley. The first solo flight was to come on 17 February in Whitley, K8938, with Sgt Emery.

The flight were to expand to normal bomber training missions as Turner got used to the Whitley, and consisted of cross-country flights, bombing and air firing flights. He 'bombed' Newcastle upon Tyne on 5 June, flying Whitley, K8978, and carried out air firing practice off South Shields on 20 June In K8984. He also made a number of flights around this time in an Avro Anson and became paired with his permanent co-pilot, F/O Anthony Colin Peach. He made a flight back to his former airfield of Usworth on 24 June, and made an overnight stay. Although he is photographed with 607 Squadron in their official squadron photograph, taken at Abbotsinch in August 1939, there is no entry in his logbook as to how or why he was there. It is presumed he made the flight to Abbotsinch on one of the days left blank in his logbook, not an unusual occurrence in Britain at the time.

With the outbreak of war, training flights were increased on 51 Squadron. Turner records that he was on a reconnaissance flight of Bremen, the Ruhr and Rheims on 27 September 1939. He recorded his first operational flight against the enemy on 23 January 1940, merely stating that it was in 'Whitley N9045 – night bombing mission. On 19 March 1940, the RAF mounted an all-night bombing attack against the German seaplane bases at Sylt. A number of RAF bombers were to take part in the offensive and Turner was to lead his flight of Whitleys from Dishforth to play their part, with Turner flying Whitley, 1408.[2] Turner was merely to record the attack as 'Bombing – Sylt'. For his actions in this raid, Turner was awarded the DFC. A.V.M C.F.A. Portal also mentioned him in dispatches on 19 May 1940 for his gallant and distinguished service, while he attended the investiture of his DFC, on 2 April. Flying Whitley 1408 once more on 11 April 1940, Turner recorded that he bombed a ship near Skaggerak, while on 16 April he failed to see the target in an attack on Oslo, and was to report 'light flak' while on a raid to Aalborg on 22 April.

On the night of 19 May 1940, Turner took off from Dishforth at 8.20 p.m., at the head of four Whitleys. The aircraft were to form up with others and carry out a bombing raid against oil refineries near Hanover. He was later to record that he experienced heavy flak during the raid.[3] His Whitley, MH-K, K1407, was severely damaged during the attack and came down near Ludwigshaven.[4] All of the crew managed to escape the aircraft and were taken prisoner. Turner was eventually taken to Dulag Luft, near Frankfurt, prior to being moved to Spangenberg. Prior to the beginning of the war, section 'Y' of MI9 trained men in the use of codes, the idea being that, if captured, they could send coded messages

Dudley Craig (left) and Willy Turner (second left) at Stalag Luft III, *c.*1943. (Family of Dudley Craig)

within normal letters back to Britain. In early 1940, Turner was one of only four men in captivity who was trained in the use of such codes. The others were Wing Commander H.M.A. Day, F/O John Gillies and Lieutenant Commander John Casson R.N. During his time in Germany from 1940–1945, Turner was to have many adventures as a PoW. On the night of 15 January 1942, he attempted to walk out of the gates of Stalag Luft 1 near Barth, dressed as a German guard. This attempted escape was made in company with his former 607 Squadron pupil pilot and friend, Dudley Craig. However, the two were stopped before they could clear the gate. The event is recorded in photographs of the time. The pair were later photographed in a group together in Stalag Luft III at Sagan, *c.*1943. p 130

The remainder of Turner's PoW life was spent sending codes via letters back to Britain, as well as passing on the code to other PoWs. With the end of hostilities, Turner was returned to Britain. The war may have been over; however, Turner was still a serving pilot in the RAF. He began his flying career once more with a course at 7 Flying Instructors School (FIS) at Uperavon. This was followed by a period at RAF Moreton-in-Marsh, flying the Vikers Wellington with 21 OTU. From flying Wellingtons, Turner then moved to 16 OTU at RAF Cottesmore, where he flew the fastest aircraft he had so far – the Mosquito. His first flight in a Mosquito TV 976 was with Sqdn Ldr Goodman as pilot, and he made his first solo Mosquito flight in Mosquito T III RR292, ending his course on 21 August 1946.

From what had been probably the fastest aircraft Turner had flown so far, he moved onto the biggest, flying a selection of Lancasters and Lincolns. Flying his first solo in a

Lincoln was on 17 September 1946 when he flew Lincoln 'D'. Turner was once again mentioned in dispatches on 31 January 1947, for distinguished service. During this time, Turner carried out his first flight to Gibraltar, on 16 November 1948 in Avro Anson, P362. He also managed to increase his 'types' flown in when he flew in a Lockheed Neptune with Commander Gage, USN, in a flight on 16 January 1949.

From January 1951, Turner began a series of flights in the largest aircraft he had flown so far, the Short Sunderland. From their base at Calshot they flew to the Mediterranean and the Far East. From August, through September and October 1952, he flew a variety of aircraft including Sunderlands and Harvards from Hong Kong. Turner was awarded the Coronation Medal in 1953 and, adding to his diversity of aircraft flown, managed a flight in a Westland Whirlwind helicopter on 19 April 1956. Turner's flying career came to a end in 1957 with his retirement from the RAF with the rank of Group Captain, and he made his final flight in Avro Anson, number 363.

Now officially retired from RAF service, Turner returned to Somerset where he took over management of the family farm. With little practical experience of farming, Willy Turner embarked on a full-time course to improve his farming skills. A modern bypass, with its compulsory purchases, finally put an end to Turner's farming career. Willy Turner died on 26 June 1976.

SAMUEL EDWARD SPROT

Samuel Edward Sprot, commonly known as 'Ted', was the second son of Colonel Hereward Sprot, landowner and coalmine owner of Woodlands Hall, Knitley, near the County Durham town of Consett. Samuel Sprot was born around 1913 and, as his father owned other estates in Scotland, including Strathvithe in Fife and Garnkirk in Lanarkshire, he may have been born on one of those. To further complicate matters, Colonel Sprot changed the family name from Sadler to Sprot by deed pole in 1931. His mother, Lady Sprot, was killed in a motor accident and, as Hereward was to succeed as head of the estates, it is thought he had to change his name to keep the Sprot name as head of the family estates. Although Hereward and some of his sons attended Cambridge, there is no trace of Samuel attending. It is known that Samuel had trouble with his legs in early life, undergoing several operations; this may have hampered his academic life.

Hereward Sprot owned, or part-owned, a number of coalmines in the Lanchester and Bishop Auckland area of County Durham, and Samuel Sprot also worked in the business as a mining engineer. Hereward Sprot had seen much service with the Dragoon Guards during the First World War and also, in later years, as commanding officer of the 9th Battalion Durham Light Infantry (DLI) TA. Samuel Sprot had been a frequent visitor at the drill hall and TA centre, and harboured ambitions to join the ranks of the '9th' as soon as possible. However, over the years Samuel had undergone a series of operations which had weakened his legs. On facing the medical examination for the Army, Samuel was deemed as unfit for service as an infantryman.

The Sprot family was actively involved in helping the unemployed and underprivileged of the area, and none more so than Samuel Sprot, who was instrumental in his work within a camp, set up in the grounds of Woodlands Hall by students of Trinity Hall, Cambridge. Away from the mining industry, Samuel Sprot was a keen aviator. Both he and his elder brother, Alexander Hereward, held 'A' licences as qualified pilots and both were members of Newcastle Aero Club, then based at Cramlington Aerodrome, Northumberland. Samuel was a keen builder of both gliders and aeroplanes, having built at least one of each with another half completed in a building at Woodlands Hall.

Bringing his keenness to join the TA together with his ability as a pilot and interest in the building of aircraft, Samuel Sprot decided to join the Auxiliary Air Force and 607 Squadron was based reasonably close at Usworth. After applying, Samuel Sprot was accepted and was gazetted as a pilot officer on 29 August 1934. He was also approved as the squadron accountant officer at this time.[1] The following month he flew with the squadron to its first annual summer camp at RAF Leuchars, not far from his father's estate in Fife.

Shortly after lunch on Wednesday 24 April 1935, Samuel Sprot and his brother decided to go flying, the latter being an officer in the Royal Artillery at home on Easter leave at the time. As their father also shared their interest in flying, they invited him as well. However, due to work commitments, their father had to decline the invitation, and so the two brothers set off for Newcastle Aero Club at Cramlington, where the pair were members. The two then made the flight in a 'Moth Comet'[2] to Woodlands Hall, Alexander acting as pilot. It is not clear if the brothers planned to make a landing at Woodlands Hall or just a few passes. However, on the approach to Woodlands Hall, the pilot lost control of the aircraft and it nose-dived into a field on their father's estate.

The aircraft crashed close to the family home – in fact so close that it was the family household staff that were first to arrive on the scene of the accident. With great difficulty they managed to extricate the two pilots from the tangled wreckage that, moments before, had been the Moth. An ambulance arrived on the scene and the two brothers were taken to the Richard Murray Hospital at Blackhall. Soon after their admission, however, Samuel Sprot was pronounced dead and Alexander was in a critical condition. An inquest, for identification purposes, was opened on Friday 26 April. The body of Samuel Sprot was then transported north to St Andrews, Fife, where, after a private family service, it was interred within the family vault in Dunino Church, Fife, on Saturday 27 April. A memorial service for the locals who knew Samuel Sprot was held that day at Lanchester Parish Church.

Although described as a 'Moth Comet', the aircraft flown by the brothers Sprot was, in fact, a de Havilland Moth DH 60G Gypsy Moth. This error in the name may well be put down to the fact that the Moth DH 60G Gypsy Moth was built by the same company, de Havilland, that was to build the Comet Racers that had taken part in the MacRobertson Air Race from England to Australia in 1934. Only six months separated the events and the name 'Comet' could still have been fresh in the mind of the press. The Gypsy Moth was a common and popular aircraft of the day; it was described by de Havilland in much the same way as a popular car of today. Anyone with garage space could own one and it could easily be towed behind a car if its wings were removed. It was also the same make and model as that flown by Amy Johnson on her record-breaking flight from Croydon to Australia in 1930. Information from Air Britain claims that the aircraft was about to land at Woodlands Hall when it crashed. The Gypsy Moth was registered as G-ABRD, number 1877 and operated by Newcastle Aero Club. Reports in the local press that the aircraft was a 'tangled wreck' may have been a bit exaggerated. Gypsy Moth G-ABRD was, at a later date, repaired and put back into service. With the onset of the Second World War, Gypsy Moth G-ABRD was re-numbered as AW 134 and pressed into RAF service. The end of Gypsy Moth G-ABRD came on 11 August 1942, when it was finally struck off charge, possibly as the result of an accident.[3]

GEORGE DUDLEY CRAIG

George Dudley Craig was born on 13 September 1914, in Bangkok, Siam. He was the only son of R.D. Craig and Sarah Louise, *née* Wilkinson. Craig Senior had arrived in Bangkok as part of the Diplomatic Corps but later became a legal advisor to the King Vajiravudh – also known as Rama VI, the artistic King of Siam. Education for Dudley Craig was carried out back in England, and he attended Aysgarth School in north-west Yorkshire. Winchester was to follow before a move to Pembroke College, the third oldest college in Cambridge. While there, Dudley Craig gained a degree and a MA in Law Studies.

Home for Dudley Craig was Hexham, a market town in south Northumberland and home of more than a few pilots who were to serve on 607 Squadron. In the latter half of 1936, Dudley, as he was known to one and all, joined the ranks of the AAF and 607 Squadron in particular. He was to make his first flight in Hawker Hart K6482, on 1 November 1936. This was his air experience flight with the squadron adjutant, Flt Lt 'Minnie' Manton. It was the following year that Craig was gazetted as a pilot officer in 607 Squadron, on 28 May 1937, with his training commencing on 1 May. On this day, Craig made his first dual flight in Avro Tutor, K2364, and was to make his first solo in the same aircraft on 26 April 1937. He was to gain his 'wings' on 13 November 1937 when he flew Hawker Hart K6482, the same aircraft in which he had made his very first flight. Still flying the two-seat Hawker Demons, Craig's regular passenger/air gunner around this time was aircraftman Charles Edward English, later to carve his own niche in aviation history as a pilot on 85 Squadron.

607 Squadron were equipped with the Gloster Gladiator at the end of 1938, and Dudley Craig made his first flight on the type on 8 January when he flew Gloster Gladiator, K8030, carrying out circuits and bumps. At the Empire Flying Day of that year, he took part as a member of the attacking force when he carried out dive-bombing attacks on the airfield in Gladiator, K7999. During this period, Craig flew Gladiator 'L' on a regular basis, and he posed with this aircraft and his ground crew at the annual summer camp at Abbotsinch in 1939. World events were to bring a hasty end to the summer camp of that year, and Craig was embodied into the RAF on 27 September 1939. With the onset of the Second World War, Craig was soon to be in action. Flying from RAF Acklington,

Northumberland, on 17 October, Craig was part of the section that successfully engaged a Do 18 flying boat off the Northumberland coast.

Dudley Craig was to fly with the squadron to France, and his part in the Battle of France and the following Battle of Britain is recorded in the main part of the text. Craig was to stay with 607 Squadron until December 1940. The squadron was moved to Turnhouse for a rest as well as rebuilding of the squadron, and Craig was moved across Turnhouse airfield where he began his duties as a supernumery (Ops duties) on 15 December 1940. After his short 'rest' away from the squadron, Craig was returned to 607 Squadron on 17 March 1941 as the new commanding officer, the squadron at that time being based at Skitten, near Wick. However, things were changing, and 607 Squadron was re-equipped with the Hawker Hurricane 2A and moved once more, this time to Castletown, on 27 July. Craig led his squadron south to Martlesham on 20 August 1941. From Martlesham, Craig trained his men in low-level tactics using the range at Orfordness.

Craig was to begin leading his squadron on offensive patrols from 18 September, this first raid being in company with the Tangmere Wing as they escorted Blenheims to the Belgian coast. The raid was not deemed a great success, as they lost A. J. Beales. A further change came on 11 October – the squadron was again re-equipped, this time with Hawker Hurricane 2Bs, making them the first Hurri-bomber unit. Craig carried out the first Hurri-bomber mission on 30 October, when, along with Sgt Lees, they successfully attacked a transformer at Tingry. On 2 November, flying as one of a section of four led by Flt Lt Slade of 615 Squadron, Craig saw Slade shot down when he failed to spot flak ships near Ostend. Sgt Lees was also shot down during this raid. If luck had been bad on 2 November, it was to prove worse two days later. Craig was leading the squadron as it made an attack on Le Touquet Airfield. For some reason, Craig dropped his bombs early, alongside a rail track. Flying low after clearing the airfield, his Hurricane 'L' was hit by intense light flak. The hurricane cleared the town of Le Touquet, then turned across the bay and ditched into the shallow waters. Craig was taken prisoner.

Dudley Craig began his captivity as PoW number 669 at Dulag Luft, the holding camp near Frankfurt. Always referred to as the 'camera whiz-kid', Craig took a number of photographs while in this camp, and judging by the amount he took, security there was not all it might have been [1] From Dulag Luft, Craig was sent to Stalag Luft 1 at Barth. It was at Barth that he met up once more with his former flying instructor from 607 Squadron, Willy Turner. On 15 January 1942, Craig and Turner teamed up to walk out of Stalag Luft 1's main gate dressed as German guards, but the attempt failed.[2]

From Stalag Luft 1, Craig was sent on to Stalag Luft 111, the old camp, before removal to Offlag XX1b at Schubin. Once again, Craig's camera was in evidence and his photographs show other former members of 607 Squadron in Schubin, among them Bobby Pumphrey and Joe Kayll. It was while at Schubin that Craig was involved in another escape attempt. A tunnel was constructed, its entrance in a lavatory, and thirty-three prisoners managed to escape. Craig and Harry 'Wings' Day were the final two to make the escape bid. With only a few Polish phrases on the back of a cigarette packet, the pair began to walk through Poland. 'Wings' Day was suffering from jaundice at the time and

Dudley Craig (left) and Willy Turner – an attempt to escape from Stalag Luft I, 1942.
(Family of Dudley Craig)

the pair were relieved when, after two days on the run, a young Polish boy offered them help, taking them to a 'safe' building so that they could hide until his return. The two escapees fell into a relieved, deep sleep only to be awakened suddenly later. Their young Polish boy had returned as promised, but with the German guards. They later found out that the young Polish boy was part of the local Hitler Youth organization. The two prisoners were returned to Schubin to face their punishment.

Dudley Craig was next moved to Stalag Luft III at Sagan, the new camp. Whilst there, Craig was involved in the camp's escape activities, working on the intelligence side. It was while at Stalag Luft III that the 'Great Escape' took place, which resulted in the shooting of fifty prisoners. Although escaping did not end there, it had a calming effect on those left. It was during this time that Craig put all his spare time to use in furthering his law studies, passing his finals while in Stalag Luft III, courtesy of the Red Cross and the Luftwaffe.

As the Russian forces began to close on Stalag Luft III, the PoWs were force-marched in the opposite direction, eventually ending up in Lukenwalde, from where they were flown back to England. Craig was mentioned in dispatches on 25 December 1945. On 23 July 1946 he was awarded an OBE in recognition of his work carried out behind the wire as a PoW. When the AAF was reformed after the war, now with the prefix 'Royal', Craig was one of those who were to rejoin the ranks, as a Flight Lieutenant on 30 May 1947. However, his flying days were over and he accepted a post in the RAAF Secretarial Branch and was gazetted on 10 October 1947. Later, he was with the Fighter Control Branch at Newcastle. Back in civilian life, Craig became a partner in a law firm in Newcastle upon Tyne. He died in 1974.

LAUNCELOT EUSTACE SMITH

Launcelot Eustace Smith was born in 1909, the son of Clarence Dalrymple and Cicely Smith of Hexham, Northumberland. Launcelot Eustace, known in later life as 'Launce', was the younger son in the family, the home of which was at Lough Brow, Dipton Road, in the market town of Hexham. Clarence Dalrymple was an OBE and a known Justice of the Peace. Well known in local business, he was also a chairman of Consett Iron Company Ltd and was on the local board of the Royal Insurance Company. He held a directorship on the London North Easter Railways (LNER) as well as the Smith's Dock ship repairing company. It is probably with the Smith's Dock company that the Smith family is most well known. The chairman of that company was Launcelot Eustace Smith, the twin brother of Clarence Dalrymple and the uncle of Launce. Launce's grandfather was Thomas Eustace Smith, the MP for Tynemouth for some twenty years. Education for the younger Launce Smith was by way of Marlborough School, followed by Cambridge. Launce Smith was to join the Tyneside engineering company of C. and A. Parsons.

Launce Smith joined the Auxiliary Air Force sometime in 1932. The squadron had only come into existence in 1930, with the first pilots arriving in 1932. Smith is recognized as being the first officer candidate. The first mention of him is made on 3 December 1932. On this day a Westland Wapiti and two Avro 504Ns arrived on the squadron. These, along with a Gypsy Moth that had arrived earlier, were to assist in the training of Leslie Runciman, already an experienced civil pilot, and training *ab initio* for Smith and Jim Vick.[1] It was not until July 1933 that Launce Smith was gazetted as a pilot officer, reaching the standard demanded for an 'A' licence during the summer of that year.

Launce Smith is present in many surviving photographs, both formal and informal. One of the latter shows a still sleeping Smith after his bed had been pulled from his tent at the 1937 summer camp. Another shows him at the bar during one of the squadron's informal get-togethers at the Eldon Grill, a well-known Newcastle bar at the time, now renamed as the Charles Grey (named after the Northumberland reformer whose monument stands in the same Eldon Square). Smith also appears prominently in a photograph of the sports events at the summer camp, as well as all the pre-war group photographs. Smith tends to stick out in the photographs, as he was a tall figure standing above most of the other squadron pilots.

Smith was promoted to the rank of Flying Officer on 3 June 1935, and the following year he married Patricia Lydia Frances Doyne, elder daughter of the late Major W.M. Doyne, formerly of the 21st Lancers. Launce's future wife was also the niece of his uncle, Launcelot Eustace Smith, the two getting married from the senior Launcelot's home at Piper Close, Corbridge. The wedding took place in St Andrew's Church, Corbridge. While the ceremony was carried out, a lone Westland Wapiti, the pilot's name unrecorded, flew low over the church in salute. Among the twelve ushers was John Sample, representing the squadron. The wedding took place on the same day as the squadron's annual inspection by the Air Officer Commanding. The wedding was followed by a honeymoon in the south of France and, on return to Northumberland, the newly married Smiths moved into a new home at Slaley, to the south of Hexham.

With the Munich crisis, 607 Squadron was absorbed into the RAF, on 27 September 1938. All squadron personnel were obliged to make use of the station barrack huts at Usworth, already a little cramped. However, the conditions were not to be endured for long. With no mobilization ordered, the squadron was stepped down from its war footing and disembodied once more, on 11 October 1938. Launce Smith was promoted to the rank of Acting Squadron Leader and, with the departure of Leslie Runciman, now on the general list, Smith was appointed commanding officer of 607 Squadron. After being the squadron's first pilot trainee, Smith was the first officer, from those part-timers picked by Leslie Runciman, to take command of 607 Squadron. It was as commanding officer that Smith led 607 Squadron to what was to be its last summer camp before the outbreak of hostilities. Smith led 607 Squadron up the coast of Northumberland and on to Abbotsinch, home of 602 (City of Glasgow) Squadron, via RAF Turnhouse. However, once again news of hostilities with Germany dominated and then erupted into war, cutting short the camp, and 607 Squadron returned to its war station at RAF Usworth. Squadron and men were once more embodied into the RAF.

Launce Smith next led his Gladiators north to RAF Acklington, arriving shortly after dawn on 10 October. If Usworth had been a little cramped, Acklington was to be worse. Already at Acklington were 609 and 152 Squadrons. 609 Squadron was operational by day only, while 152 Squadron was still a new squadron and therefore non-operational. On arrival, 607 Squadron found that it was the fully operational squadron at Acklington, and was to maintain one flight at readiness while the other was to remain available. Training was stepped up once more, as were the standing patrols, and there was regular flying practice as well as gunnery practice at a target marker in nearby Druridge Bay. During this period of uncertainty, the squadron was under the impression that it was to be sent to France on short notice.

The uncertainty came to an end on 13 November 1939; Launce Smith led 607 Squadron south to Croydon as a preparatory move to France. The final hurdle, held up for two days due to bad weather, went ahead on 15 November. 607 Squadron left Croydon in company with 615 Squadron on the last leg that would take them to Merville, France. The move of the formation was witnessed by Winston Churchill and prompted from him the comment that the formation was, 'The worst equipped units in Fighter Command'. The remark was aimed at the variety of both civil as well as military aircraft which made up the formation, rather than the quality of the fighter squadrons. A number of civil transport aircraft were drafted in to carry supplies and the ground personnel.

His Majesty King George VI made a visit to France on 6 December to visit the squadrons of the Air Component, the inspection of the squadrons taking place at Seclin, a few miles south of Lille. Launce Smith and John Sample flew their Gladiators into Seclin on 5 December for a dress rehearsal of the visit, and returned the following day for the inspection itself. Rain, which had persisted for a few days, eventually cleared, leaving a misty Seclin as King George VI arrived with the Duke of Gloucester and duly inspected the squadrons and their crews.

As well as the regular patrols carried out during this time, there were a number of co-operation flights carried out with other aircraft. Launce Smith led a section, consisting of Joe Kayll and Tony Forster, on 7 December on a co-operation flight with Lysanders. However, due to the bad weather, the Lysanders failed to appear. Smith led his section to Vitry to take a look at the airfield on his way back to Merville. The squadron was due to move from Merville to Vitry a few days later, and arrived there on 13 December 1939. Smith was to lead another section on Lysander co-operation on 19 December. On this occasion the section consisted of Joe Kayll and Will Gore, the flight taking place in the area of Douai, and on this occasion the Lysanders managed to turn up. With bad weather still prevalent into December, Launce Smith departed France on 21 December 1939, and returned to Northumberland for Christmas leave.

On his return to France, Smith was to find the number of patrols had been stepped up. Photographs survive from this period which show Lance Smith in France. A group of pilots, including Will Whitty, Tony Forster and Peter Parrott, has Smith at its centre. He also makes an appearance in the photograph which shows former CO Leslie Runciman's visit to the squadron. Also in evidence are the boggy conditions of the airfields of France during the winter of 1939–40, with duckboards laid out in front of the hut entrances.

When the German Blitzkrieg broke through into France on 10 May 1940, Launce Smith was once more on leave. He made a return to France but missed the first two or three days of the air fighting. His first recorded flight in the Battle of France came on 13 May. A patrol, on this occasion led by Francis Blackadder, was slightly overdue, and Smith was concerned about the extent that he took off in Hurricane P3448,

AF-H, taking with him Bob Weatherill and Tony Dini. The threesome encountered a formation of Me 109s along the way and carried out an attack. Both Tony Dini and Launce Smith claimed 'kills', although Smith identified his 'kill' as a He 112. In the combat, Smith's Hurricane had suffered more than a few hits and returned somewhat damaged.

Launce Smith led a formation on 15 May, made up of five Hurricanes from 607 Squadron, and six Hurricanes from 615 Squadron led by Joe Kayll. The formation was to provide escort to a group of Blenheims that were to attack the bridges over the Meuse. While flying over the area of Dinant at around 11,000ft, the Hurricanes were bounced by the Stab flight of III/JG 52, consisting of Me 110s and 109s. In the fighting which followed, Hurricane P2870 fell away from the fighting, taking Smith to his death. One unnamed source stated that Smith's Hurricane was hit by ground fire. Francis Blackadder, not one of the formation on this day, stated that he thought Smith had gone to the aid of some Fairey Battles.[2]

The body of Launce Smith was never knowingly recovered, and is probably buried somewhere in France as an 'unknown airman'. His name is recorded on the Runnymede Memorial for missing airmen. On the Hexham road leading out of Corbridge lies the cemetery of St Andrews. Just inside the main gate stands the war memorial to those of the parish who fell in both wars. Facing the gateway are the names of those who fell in the Second World War. On this slab is the name of Launcelot Eustace Smith.

JOHN SAMPLE

John Sample was born in 1913, the first son of Thomas Norman and Kate Isabel Sample. Thomas Norman, a former soldier, was part-owner of the Newcastle-based shipping line, Richley, Holverson & Sample, working from their office in Milburn House, Newcastle upon Tyne. The family home was Longhirst Grange, an ex-farmhouse on the outskirts of the village of Longhirst, some 2 miles north of Morpeth, Northumberland. The baptism of John Sample took place at St John's Church, Longhirst, on 27 February 1913. The first few years of John Sample's education must have been carried out by private tutor, as there is no record of him attending any local school. Academic life for Sample was to begin at Aysgarth School, Bedale, in the Pennine district of North Yorkshire.

Among its 'old boys', Aysgarth School was to have no less than five who were to fly in the Battle of Britain: Clive Hilken, Hugh Dundas, Dudley Craig, Joe Kayll and John Sample. A plaque was erected to this effect in 2000 to mark the sixtieth anniversary of the Battle of Britain. The headmaster was known to have drummed into his boys, 'the importance of acting rather than talking'. Among the 'old boys', who seemed to take this literally, was Richard Meinertzhagen. Later, as an intelligence officer with the Directorate of Military Operations for the War Office, Meinertzhagen was credited with leading the rescue of Grand Duchess Tatiana Nicolaevena Romanov after the Russian revolution of 1918.[1]

John Sample left Aysgarth in 1925 and moved to Lansing School, Brighton. Sample was later to study as a land agent and became a member of the Land Agents' Society as well as the Surveyors' Institute. It is thought that John Sample worked for a short period for a firm of land agents in Haltwhistle, Northumberland, as part of his training. What is known for certain is that Sample next went to work as joint agent to his uncle, William Collings Sample, land agent to the Dukes of Portland, working from his office in Bothal Castle, Northumberland.

Among his many attributes, John Sample was musical and was accomplished in playing the concertina, accordion and the Northumbrian pipes. He was to win competitions for playing the latter and also played with Jack Armstrong, one-time piper to the Duke of Northumberland, in a radio broadcast of the period. Sample was also an above-average shot with both rifle and revolver, and a shooting range near his house was used for practice. In later years he was to win county competitions as well as leading an RAF team to victory at Bisley.

Sample was to join 607 Squadron and was gazetted on 27 April 1934 as a pilot officer, and was the fifth pilot candidate to join the squadron, obtaining his flying badge on 4 August 1934. Sample appears in all of the official group photographs of the pre-war period and also in many unofficial ones. Perhaps one of the better ones is an air-to-air shot of Sample flying Hawker Demon K3800. Sample was later to be the squadron's training officer and signed himself as F/O John Sample OC 'T' Flight. He was promoted to the rank of Flight Lieutenant on 7 June 1939, and took over from Launce Smith as the commanding officer of 'B' Flight later that year.

At the beginning of the war, John Sample led a section which claimed a Do 18 on 17 October 1939, giving the squadron its first kill. In November the squadron was to move south to France to take up its position with the Air Component. During the early months of the French campaign, Sample took command of the squadron on more than one occasion, standing in for Launce Smith when he was away on leave. He was also to assume command of 61 Fighter Wing Servicing Unit – again, in place of an officer on leave, on this occasion, Sqdn Ldr Harvey, OC 615 Squadron. During this period, John Sample also took his place on the 'Blighty' patrols, as well as the usual standing patrols and the co-operation flights with the Lysanders. When the fighting got underway in earnest with the Blitzkrieg of 10 May, Sample was in the thick of it, managing to claim two He 111s before having to vacate his Hurricane due to it being covered in oil. Making a heavy landing by parachute, he sprained both ankles and his flying was temporarily ended. However, with the demise of both Launce Smith and George Fidler, Sample assumed command of 607 Squadron in its dying days in France. A few photographs of Sample survive from this period, some in full flying gear, and others when he was more relaxed.[2]

With the return of 607 Squadron to England, John Sample departed to take command of 504 Squadron, initially based at Wick and later at Castletown. It was during this period that Sample was awarded the DFC, on 4 June 1940, for his actions in France. After building up 504 Squadron, which had also suffered in France, and training the new pilots, Sample led 504 Squadron south to Hendon, taking up their position in the Battle of Britain. Sample left a radio broadcast as part of his legacy in the events of 15 September 1940. Although one of his sergeant pilots, Ray Holmes, is feted as being the victor over a Dornier Do 17, supposedly en route to bomb Buckingham Palace, this was not the case.

At least another seven aircraft had attacked this Do 17 before Ray Holmes came along, and among them was John Sample – all had their share in its demise. Later the same day, Sample successfully attacked another Do 17, the hapless bomber eventually crashing onto Barnehurst golf course. Like other squadrons in the Battle of Britain, 504 Squadron took its share of losses and the time came for them to relocate out of the battle zone for a rest. Firstly, they were to move to Filton in defence of that area before moving on to Exeter. Now, with the air defence dying down and the squadron located nearer the coast, offensive patrols were flown across France into early 1941. In March 1941, Sample, who had now been flying continuously for over six years, was taken off flying for a 'rest', and was posted to group HQ as a controller.

21 September 1941 saw the birth of a new unit, 137 Squadron. The squadron was to fly the Westland Whirlwind, the second and only other squadron to do so. The first squadron to fly the aircraft was 263 Squadron, and both squadrons were to share the same airfield of Charmy Down. The airfield was close enough to France for the aircraft to carry out ground attacks against the enemy. Sample, making a return to flying, was to lead 137 Squadron. Sample slowly but surely formed 137 Squadron into a fighting unit, and within a month one flight was operational and involved in attacks over France. While working on the second flight, Sample was involved in a flying accident, when one of the aircraft in his section collided with him on 28 October 1941. The other aircraft managed to limp

Remains of the Hurricane of Sgt E.A.S. Parris, shot down on 21 September 1941. The Hurricane crashed into the square at Montreuil Sur Mer, northern France. (Guillaume Rault)

back to base. However, Whirlwind P7053 spun out of control and crashed into a cowshed on Manor Farm, Englishcombe. Sample may have had difficulty extricating himself from the doomed Whirlwind. As a result, he was too low for his parachute to deploy properly and he crashed onto the roof of the farmhouse of Manor Farm with fatal results.

John Sample was buried within the family plot in the churchyard of St Andrew's Church, Bothal, a mere stone's throw from the office where he worked as a land agent in Bothal Castle. His headstone is part of the family plot and his grave bears no CWGC headstone. Sample is remembered on the Battle of Britain Memorial, London. Nearer home, however, is a different story. His name appears on a wooden plaque, dedicated to those of 607 Squadron who were awarded honours in the Second World War, in part of the North East Aviation Museum, formerly RAF Usworth. His name on the Longhirst War Memorial was the only one added for those who fell in the conflict. His mother, Kate Isabel Sample, commissioned a silver cup in memory of her son in 1949; the cup is still awarded annually in the Northumbrian Pipers' Society.

The John Sample Cup, presented to the Northumbrian Pipers' Society by Mrs Kate Isabel Sample in memory of her son, John. The cup is awarded annually in Northumbrian piping competitions. (Morpeth Bagpipe Museum)

WILLIAM FRANCIS BLACKADDER

William Francis Blackadder was born on 23 January 1913, the son of architect Robert Blackadder and his wife, Gwen. The young William Francis, later known as Francis, attended Merchiston School, Edinburgh. This was to be followed by Grenville and Caius College, Cambridge University. On leaving academic life, Francis Blackadder began work with the Anchor Shipping Line of Newcastle upon Tyne, the shipping line owned and run by the Runciman family. It is perhaps with the Anchor Line that Francis Blackadder's interest in flying began. Leslie Runciman had an interest in flying, later becoming the 607 Squadron CO, and was also an ex-Cambridge graduate.

Francis Blackadder was to join the Auxiliary Air Force in January 1936. He was gazetted as a pilot officer on 1 June 1936. His first flight had come on 19 January 1936, the familiarisation flight flown in Avro 504, K2387, with Flt Lt Singer. Blackadder was to record this flight as 'suitability'. A further flight in the same aircraft was carried out on 23 February, with Blackadder recording this as 'Prospective candidate' in his logbook. He was accepted for flying training and training proper got under way with three flights on 15 March 1936.

Most of Blackadder's flights were carried out with Flt Lt Manton as instructor; however, P/O Bartlett, the assistant adjutant and flying instructor, as well as John Sample and Launce Smith, also accompanied him on occasion. Blackadder flew his first solo on 29 September 1936, in Hawker Demon K5686. With the beginning of 1937, Blackadder was flying cross-country flights ranging away from the vicinity of Usworth. His first was to Turnhouse, where his return journey was took him down the coastal route. As he carried out more cross-country flights, his confidence grew. However, it was slightly dented on 28 March 1937. That morning, Blackadder was flying Demon K5689 on a cross-country flight via Falstone to Wooler. Approaching the Cheviot Hills, the high ground between England and Scotland and graveyard of many aircraft, he was forced back by increasingly low cloud. On his return, the Demon overshot the runway and tipped onto its nose. Blackadder must have put the experience behind him, however, as he qualified for his' wings' on 25 April 1937.

He was in charge of ten men who travelled to London to take up street-lining duties on Constitution Hill on 10 May 1937, the day of the coronation of King George VI. For his part in the ceremony, Blackadder was awarded the Coronation Medal on 29 May. In August, it was the annual tea party held by Lord Londonderry. Blackadder flew to Newtonards as a passenger in Demon K5692, with Ralph Carr-Ellison as the pilot on both the outward and inward journeys. The annual summer camp was held from 15 August, and Blackadder records that he flew down to Rochford in Demon K5692, by way of Waddington. A flight in one of the squadron's aircraft was much prized among the ground crew, being both easier and swifter than the normal road or rail transport. On this occasion, LAC Armstrong was in the back seat of Blackadder's Demon while LAC White took the set on the return journey, on 28 August.

After the return from summer camp, night flying was given priority. Francis Blackadder's first night flight was in Tutor K4825 with Flt Lt Manton. Practice was to continue in other areas as well, mainly formation and aerobatics. At this time, Blackadder records that he took part in a battle climb to 15,000ft, his passenger on this occasion being Aircraftman Charles English. Charles English was later to fly with 85 Squadron in the Battle of Britain. There now followed a halt to Blackadder's training programme, due to 'business'. Francis Blackadder was not to fly again until the following April. It was, however, during this period, on 19 March 1938, that Blackadder was capped for Scotland, when he took part in the Scottish rugby defeat of England.

The next important step for Blackadder came on Saturday 7 January 1939. On this day he had his first flight in the squadron's newly acquired aircraft, the Gloster Gladiator, making a short familiarisation flight in K8030. This was the same Gladiator that Dudley Craig was to make his first flight in the following day. The next day, Blackadder was flying Gladiator K7999 on formation practice with Dudley Craig flying K9969. Even though the new Gladiators were much sought after on the squadron, there were still Hawker Demons on the squadron strength. Blackadder gave an air experience flight to various passengers on 31 July 1939. Blackadder flew Gladiator 'F' to Abbotsinch on 12 August 1939 to take part in the annual summer camp, which was cut short due to the declaration of war. He was to fly 'F' home again on 24 August. Now back at Usworth and embodied into the RAF, Blackadder recorded his first patrol of the war on 3 September 1939, once again flying Gladiator 'F'.

The squadron was moved to Acklington on 10 October, and was on detachment to Drem by 16 October. The next main move was to France, the flight beginning on 15 November before arriving at Merville two days later. Once settled in at Merville, a routine of training and patrols was settled into. It was during this period that Francis Blackadder recorded the loss of Gladiator 'F'. This incident took place on 24 March 1940 as Harry Radcliffe carried out 'attacks' on the Gladiator that Nigel Graeme was flying. The two aircraft collided and Gladiator 'F' crashed and was burnt out. How these deaths affected the other pilots can be seen in the fact that Francis Blackadder merely recorded the demise of Gladiator 'F', noting that it killed Harry Radcliffe. Dudley Craig was to make a note in his logbook to the effect that both pilots had been carrying out simulated attacks and were killed in a mid-air collision. This is not to point out that either of the pilots, Blackadder or Craig, were right or wrong – they merely recorded things differently.

The squadron was now to be re-equipped with the Hawker Hurricane, and the new aircraft were taken over at Abbeville in April. Blackadder made his first flight on 15 April in Hurricane P2536, AF-R. He had a few test flights in this and other Hurricanes before settling with P2572, AF-F. He flew most of the patrols in the Battle of France in this aircraft. However, it appears not to have survived the French campaign, having crashed in the hands of another pilot or, more likely, just left behind when the squadron hurriedly vacated France. Certainly, this Hurricane did not make the flight back to England in the hands of Francis Blackadder. On 20 May he made the flight from Merville to Hendon in similar circumstances to Dudley Craig – in the back seat of a Douglas, flown by an unnamed pilot. Blackadder recorded in his logbook that he was 'War Weary'.

When 607 Squadron reformed at Croydon on 29 May, Blackadder was to make three flights in Hurricane P2874, testing it out. This was followed by a flight in a Hurricane of 17 Squadron, unrecorded number, from Croydon. The endurance of the flight being ten minutes was followed by the recorded comment in his logbook 'Impossible'. Blackadder then turned his attention back to P2874 as well as two other Hurricanes, before declaring P2874 his own 'F'. It was in this aircraft that he flew most of his patrols throughout the Battle of Britain. During June, he appears to have been on a tour of British bases in the company of Lord Trenchard, known as the Father of the Royal Air Force. Flights were made to various bases in a Dh 86 with F/O Jeffries recorded as pilot, these flights being carried out over the period 8–10 June. Of course, Blackadder was to feature prominently in the Battle of Britain and his exploits during this period are recorded in the main text.

Number 607 Squadron had received some punishment during its stay at Tangmere. With time for a 'rest', 607 Squadron departed from Tangmere on 10 October, and flew north to Turnhouse with detachments at Drem. A couple of weeks later, Blackadder flew Hurricane P2874 on his last flight with 607 Squadron, a flight from Usworth to Turnhouse on 24 October 1940. On his return to Turnhouse, he was attached to RAF Turnhouse (on operations) as a controller; his official posting to Turnhouse took place on 6 November. Blackadder was to fly a number of light aircraft during this period as he ferried himself around the bases of the group. He was later to move on to Prestwick, Ayr and Usworth, where he carried on the same job of controller. During this period he also carried out some public relations duties, making at least a couple of flights to Fettes College, Edinburgh. Occasionally he got to grips with the more operational aircraft, one of these being the Spitfire. Flying Spitfire R7071 to an inspection at Gilston, he performed a roll and collapsed the cockpit hood.

Francis Blackadder was next posted to 245 Squadron as its commanding officer. 245 Squadron were flying Spitfires from Aldergrove and, later, Ballyhalbert and Chilbolten. Blackadder was to remain with 245 Squadron until July 1942. On 13 July, he was posted once more to controller duties when he was seconded to 10 Group at Rudloe Manor. He was to follow this with a course at the Army Staff College, Camberley, before being transferred to HQ Fighter Command as a Wing Commander (tactics). This, in turn, was followed by a move to HQ Allied Expeditionary Forces from 28 September 1943.

In 1945, he made a return to flying duties when he took command of the Air Fighting Development Unit at Wittering from January 1945. Whilst there, he managed to fly a variety of aircraft from the Hurricane to Typhoon, as well as Spitfires, Mustangs and Tempests, while among the more unusual aircraft that he flew were the Messerschmitt Me 110 and 109 fighters. His time at Wittering was to be his last posting in the wartime RAF. He left the RAF in November 1945.

The Auxiliary Air Force had also disbanded by 15 August 1945 with the cessation of hostilities. However, due to mounting pressure the AAF was reformed in May 1946. Blackadder was to rejoin 607 Squadron in September 1946, and the squadron was now operating from its new base at RAF Ouston. Other units were now operating from Usworth, a few miles to the west of Newcastle, in Northumberland. Blackadder was mainly flying the Harvard during this time. The squadron's operational aircraft was the Spitfire, and Francis Blackadder made one of his first flights in the squadron Spitfire on 12 January 1947, when he flew Spitfire xivTZ 116 on a local flight.

607 Squadron RAAF at the annual summer camp, Lubeck, 1948.

Annual summer camps were also back on the agenda, and one of the first was to RAF Lubeck in Germany in 1948, one of the main attractions of Lubeck, militarily speaking, being its proximity to the Russian frontier in the build-up to the Cold War. Blackadder was to take on the duties of squadron adjutant during 1948, during what was to be his final year with the squadron. He recorded his last flight on 4 December 1948, when he flew Spitfire 'M' on an air test. He was finally to leave the RAAF and 607 Squadron in December 1948. His days with the RAF were not yet at an end, however, as he took command of the Northumberland Wing of the ATC, a position he held until February 1951. Francis Blackadder died in 1997.

GRAHAM ASHLEY LEONARD MANTON

Graham Ashley Leonard Manton was born on 18 June 1910 and was to join the RAF on a short service commission (general duties branch) in June 1931. Flying training was carried out at 2 Flying Training School (FTS) at RAF Digby from 13 July 1931. After completion of his flying training Manton was posted to 111 Squadron, a fighter squadron, and was on the squadron by 20 June 1932. Based at RAF Hornchurch, the squadron at that time was flying the Bristol Bulldog, and Manton was to stay with the squadron until 1934. On 29 March of that year, Manton was posted to 605 (County of Warwick) Auxiliary Squadron the squadron that was to give him his first taste of life on an Auxiliary squadron. The squadron at that time was based at its traditional home of West Bromwich. During this period, the squadron was flying the Westland Wapiti, a two-seat bomber, in the light bomber role. Manton was posted to 605 Squadron in a liaison capacity between the Auxiliary squadron and RAF Bomber Command. Manton's official capacity was that of assistant adjutant as well as some instructional duties. Manton was to depart from 605 Squadron to take a course as a flying instructor, after which he was posted to yet another Auxiliary squadron: 607 (County of Durham) Auxiliary Squadron.

Flt Lt Manton arrived at RAF Usworth on 17 July 1936, where he took up the post of adjutant and flying instructor with 607 Squadron, replacing Flt Lt N.C. Singer, who was departing to take an armament course at AAS RAF Eastchurch. One of the first trainee pilots of 607 Squadron to fly with Manton was Francis Blackadder, who was to record that he flew with Manton as instructor on 26 July 1936, and again on the 28th on a local flight in the squadron's Avro, number 1806. It was at this time that Manton seemed to acquire the nickname 'Minnie', thus becoming Minnie Manton in the photo albums of the day. Minnie Manton was also Blackadder's instructor when he mad a flight in Hawker Hart, K6482, on 1 September 1936. Francis Blackadder recorded that Manton was to fly as his instructor on a number of cross-country flights, as well as a formation flight on 24 January 1937 and an aerobatic session on 22 April. Both flights were in Hawker Hart K6482, an aircraft that seemed to be much favoured by Manton during this period. A photograph of this Hawker Hart still exists. Francis Blackadder was to record that his last flight with Manton was carried out on 14 October 1937, and this was a night flying exercise in Avro Tutor, K4825.

As a squadron adjutant, Manton's duties were wide and varied. As he was also the squadron flying instructor, he had to assist the commanding officer in the interviewing of trainee pilots. This aspect of his position meant that he flew the candidates on their familiarisation flights, and for most this flight was their very first. One of the downsides of squadron life was accidents and death. On 14 May 1937, Tim Richardson was killed in a flying accident on his return from Sutton Bridge. It was the duty of Manton, as adjutant, to attend the coroner's inquest and give evidence on behalf of the deceased. A more positive aspect was provided by the Empire Flying Day. In 1937 this was held on 19 May and, while the squadron participated in mock attacks and ground strafing, it was Minnie Manton who carried out the solo aerobatics display in one of the squadron's Hawker Demons.

One 607 Squadron pilot who had his maiden flight with Manton was Dudley Craig. He was to record his first flight as being in November 1936 when he was taken for a flight in Hawker Hart K6482, an aircraft often used by Manton – a photograph exists of this aircraft. Dudley Craig seems to have spent much of his training with Manton, flying, amongst others, Avro K2387 and his first flight in a Hawker Demon, K5688, which came on 21 February 1937. Manton also flew with Dudley Craig on his first cross-country flight to Bicester on 5 January 1937, and another flight on 22 January to RAF Hendon. Manton appears in the group photograph of 1937, taken at the annual inspection, where he sits to the left of Sqdn Ldr Runciman. He also appears in full flying gear with a pilot named 'Boz', and a more informal photograph of Manton appears with him in a relaxed pose with Bobby Pumphrey while on an

Alpine holiday in 1937. Manton was to be posted from 607 Squadron on 29 November 1937. However, before leaving, Manton was to have two flights with the new adjutant, Willy Turner. The pair flew on a test, with Willy Turner as pilot, in Magister L6109 on 10 November. On 12 November 1937, Manton flew once more with Willy Turner in Blenheim K8046. A third airman was F/O Dowland, and Turner was to describe the flight as a 'dual instruction'.

Manton was next posted to 6 Auxiliary Group, the group having just been reformed, on 1 May 1936, under the command of Air Commodore J.C. Quinnell. In June 1940, Manton was sent on a refresher course to 12 Group Pool, later 5 OUT, at the Cotswold airfield of Aston Down. Presumably this was to convert to the Hawker Hurricane, as his next posting was to 56 Squadron who were flying the Hurricane from North Weald. Manton was posted to North Weald to take command of 56 Squadron from 1 July 1940. 56 Squadron had already seen action, as they were involved in the air defence of the Dunkirk evacuation. Shortly after Manton joined 56 Squadron, the unit was to be involved in the first actions of the Battle of Britain, when the Luftwaffe attacked shipping in the English Channel. 56 Squadron were involved in the action of 13 July, when F/O Richard E.P. Brooker and Sgt James R. Cowsill were to claim Ju 87s as 'damaged', and both aircraft made forced landings in France. 56 Squadron had two Hurricanes damaged and two lost, one of these being the Hurricane of Sgt Cowsill. Manton was also to make a claim for one Ju 87 shot down. In July, Manton was to make a claim for one Me 110 shot down and again, on 24 July, he made a claim for one Me 109. The following day, in combat with Ju 87s near Dover, Manton was wounded and his Hurricane: P3479 slightly damaged. Manton was posted away fro 56 Squadron on 24 August 1940, his place being taken by Sqdn Ldr Moreton Pinfold.

Manton was next posted to RAF Manston, where he took command on 31 August, the airfield having suffered in the recent heavy bombing. The following year, Manton was promoted to the rank of Wing Commander, on 1 March, and took command of the Northolt Wing. The following month, Manton was leading the wing on a bomber escort when they were bounced and Manton was wounded. His Hurricane, Z 2492, made a force-landing near Romney. The following month he was again wounded and served a period at Colerne before being posted to Fighter HQ Belfast. Manton was later to serve on a number of staff positions, among them commanding officer of both RAF Church Fenton and RAF Coltishall, while in 1946 he was at 13 Fighter Group HQ, Inverness. Post-war, Manton was to serve with HQ Allied Air Forces at Kolsas in Oslo, Norway. On retirement from RAF service on 26 June 1960, Manton retired to Australia.

JOSEPH ROBERT KAYLL

Joseph Robert Kayll was born on 12 April 1914, the elder son of Major Joseph Pelham and Kathleen Kayll of Sunderland. Education for Joe Kayll began at Aysgarth School and this was followed by a period at Stowe School. With his studies at Stowe completed, Kayll decided to discontinue the academic life and returned to Sunderland, where he began work with the Sunderland timber company of Joseph Thompson. It was around this time that Kayll decided to serve his country on a part-time basis and to this end he chose the Auxiliary Air Force; his local unit, 607 Squadron, was based only a couple of miles from his home.

In late 1933, Joe Kayll became only the fourth officer candidate to join 607 Squadron for pilot training. He was gazetted on 9 March 1934, as a pilot officer and also gained his pilots' 'A' licence. As his experience grew, Kayll was to accompany some of the less experienced pilots on their training flights. Kayll was to fly with Dudley Craig in Avro K2364 on short training flights during July 1937, as well as a cross-country flight in Hawker Hart K6482 to Waddington on 15 August 1937. Francis Blackadder was recorded that he flew a cross-country flight to Dishforth on 6 October 1937, with Kayll in Hawker Demon K5691. Kayll was promoted to the rank of Flight Lieutenant on 1 July 1939, and shortly afterwards took command of 'A' Flight when Leslie Runciman relinquished command of the squadron.

On 13 November 1939, 607 Squadron were to fly to France with 615 (County of Surrey) Squadron. On 16 March 1940, things were to change for Joe Kayll; for the first time in his flying career he was parted from 607 Squadron when he was posted to command 615 Squadron, even though the move was not far – just across the airfield of Vitry, where 615 Squadron shared the airfield with 607 Squadron. In April, both squadrons were to move to Abbeville where they were re-equipped with the Hawker Hurricane. When the German Blitzkrieg broke through on the continent, 615 Squadron were soon in the thick of the fighting. On 15 May, Kayll was to claim two Me 110s as 'destroyed' and these were followed by a claim for a He 111 on 20 May.

With the end of the Battle of France, 615 Squadron returned to re-group at Kenley and it was from there that Kayll continued to lead 615 Squadron on patrols as well as reconnaissance flights across France for the Army. On his return to Kenley from one of these patrols, he was to find King George VI visiting the station, and Kayll was awarded the DSO and the DFC by the King for his actions in the French campaign. Kayll continued to lead 615 Squadron throughout the early part of the Battle of Britain before the squadron was withdrawn for a rest, on 28 August 1940, when the squadron flew north to Prestwick.

With the squadron rested and new pilots trained, Kayll led his men south once more on 10 October, and took up station at Northolt and later Heathrow. At the latter, Kayll was to lead patrols at wing strength of three squadrons. On the morning of 28 October 1940, Kayll was to make his last claim in the official Battle of Britain period, making a claim for a Me 109 as 'damaged' when 615 Squadron attacked the fighter escort of a raid near London. In December, Kayll was taken off flying and posted to HQ Fighter Command, his first break from flying since 1934.

Kayll was next appointed Wing Leader of the Hornchurch Wing from 2 June 1941, the wing being engaged in cross-Channel fighter sweeps. In command of RAF Hornchurch was Harry Broadhurst who, as station commander, had the right to lead the Hornchurch Wing and he exercised that right on 25 July 1941.[1] The Hornchurch Wing had met with little success on this day and was turning for home, but Harry Broadhurst made the decision to turn back to France and take another look. Leading

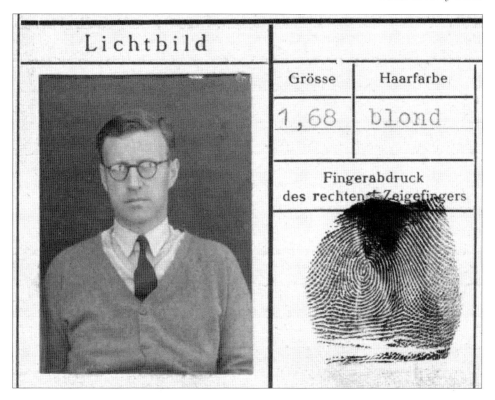

Lichtbild	Grösse	Haarfarbe
	1,68	blond

Fingerabdruck
des rechten Zeigefingers

Dudley Craig's ID card from Stalag Luft III. The photo shows Craig wearing glasses – these were passed around to give a misleading picture of escapees. (Family of Dudley Craig)

the section back across Lille, they were bounced by Me 109s. Of the four Spitfires in the section, only that of Harry Broadhurst made it back to Hornchurch. Kayll's Spitfire made a forced-landing in a field near St Omer. A photograph exists of Kayll being led away by his captors.

Like many before him and many who were to come later, Joe Kayll was to spend the rest of the war as a 'guest' of the Germans. He proceeded through Dulag Luft, Spangenberg Castle, Oflag VIb, Schubin and Stalag Luft III, surviving more than a few prison escapes along the way. Kayll was finally repatriated by the Russian forces in May 1945, and he left the RAF later the same year with the rank of Wing Commander.

Kayll was mentioned in despatches on 28 December 1945, and received an OBE on 26 July 1946 in recognition of his work as a PoW. Kayll returned to Sunderland and the family business of Joseph Thompson & Co., where he was known by the workforce as 'Mr Joe'. Now with the prefix 'Royal' added, the Royal Auxiliary Air Force came back into being on 10 December 1947. Among its first members was Kayll, who was given the honour of being 607 Squadron's first post-war commanding officer. Joe Kayll eventually retired from flying in 1951 and died in March 2000.

Notes

1. Selina Hastings, *Rosamond Lehmann: A Life*, p.74.
2. From logbooks of Willy Turner.
3. The logbooks of Willy Turner often have the letter missing from the aircraft number.
4. The entry in Willy Turner's logbook was written after the end of the war.
5. Two photographs of Willy Turner's Whitley are known to exist in Germany.
6. A number of photographs exist of Dudley Craig and Willy Turner, both in and out of their home-made German uniforms at this time. They are in the collection of Dudley Craig.
7. 607 Squadron ORB.
8. A report in the *Newcastle Journal*, 25–26 April, names the type of aircraft as a Moth Comet.
9. Malcolm Filmore and Paul McMillan via the Internet.
10. Dudley Craig's photo album has a number of photographs taken of various people and places within Dulag Luft.
11. There are around five different views of this event, with some showing the guards.
12. 607 Squadron ORB.
13. Notes provided by Francis Blackadder, courtesy of the family of Peter Dixon.
14. Michael Occleshaw, *The Romanov Conspiracies – The Romanovs And The House Of Windsor*. (Chapman's Publishers, 1993).
15. Photographs mostly appear in the photo albums and logbook of Dudley Craig.
16. The book *Hornchurch Offensive*, Vol. 2, p.17, highlights the fact that there were harsh words between Harry Broadhurst and Joe Kayll, on more than a few occasions, over who would lead the Hornchurch Wing. As usual, rank prevailed on that morning, with disastrous consequences for Joe Kayll.

CONCLUSIONS

607 Squadron was born as a result of the RAF expansion programme of the 1930s. It had not been an easy birth, as many were still against the expansion of the RAF and even more brought forth the question: why have an air force at all? Aviation was still in the novelty stage and was seen by many as an adventure, while others looked upon it as a gentleman's plaything, a pursuit carried out only by those who could afford it. Now, a new air arm was to be launched and its pilots were to come from the ranks of a certain class of men. They were to be part-timers at best, overpaid glory seekers at worst. This was the perception of the general public who swelled the ranks of the increasing numbers of air displays. The members who kept the AAF expanding originated from the same area of the squadron, adhering to the vision of Trenchard, who saw the AAF as being territorial. However, these men were a different class of men, and a different breed from the normal indigenous men of the area, their civilian careers allowing them a certain amount of freedom, even in the lean, strike-ridden years of the 1920s and into the 1930s. These men were also a different breed from their RAF counterparts, the two not sitting well together in the early years. This period was, of course, the 'glory days' of the RAF, and the AAF was pulled along with it. Pilots of both the RAF and the emerging AAF were looked upon as the 'gladiators of the sky'.

Of course, the men of the AAF differed from those of the RAF, both in men and traditions. The men of the AAF would be seen as almost lackadaisical in their approach, especially to training as servicemen. The officers of the RAF looked upon them as under trained interlopers. It is also a fact that RAF squadrons of the period were born out of long tradition, a tradition that had been born and honed in the battles of the First World War. The squadrons of the AAF, meanwhile, were new and untried and, as with all things new, they were looked upon with a jaundiced eye. With the beginning of the Second World War, however, this was to change drastically. Firstly, because the squadrons of the AAF proved their worth very quickly in the Battle of France, as they were among the first in combat. Secondly, as the war progressed attrition came into play and most squadrons began to be equipped with RAF personnel, the older, 'original' Auxiliary personnel falling victim to the war or being posted onto RAF squadrons.

Of course, all squadrons had characters among their ranks and 607 Squadron had its share of these, some of them having connections with world events. Viscount Runciman, the father of the first commanding officer of the squadron, was involved in the peace process between Britain and Germany of 1939. 607 Squadron, being an Auxiliary squadron, also had an Honorary Air Commodore. The man was, of course, Lord Londonderry, one-time

A board showing 607 Squadron pilots who were decorated, 1940. The board is held by the
N.E.A.M. Museum at Usworth. (Author)

Air Minister in the government. Later, while still providing his duties to 607 Squadron, he rubbed shoulders with various members of the German Nazi hierarchy, as well as meeting the German Chancellor, Adolf Hitler, himself. It would have been interesting to know how the pilots of 607 Squadron viewed this friendship. More than a few of the 607 Squadron personnel were to spend time behind the wire as 'guests' of Germany, and most have interesting stories to tell as a result. Certainly, one of the more interesting is that of Sqdn Ldr Willy Turner. Willy Turner was unfortunate in being shot down early in 1940. As a result, he was one of only four in German captivity with access to the MI9 codes. Sending coded letters himself, as well as teaching others in captivity, it would be interesting to know how much of PoW life as well as information about German activities was sent back to MI9, thanks to Willy Turner.

The story of 607 Squadron is to end here, although the squadron was to move on to greater things and was to play an increasing part in the war, not only in Europe but also in the Far East, as it fought against the imperial might of the Japanese. As we have already seen, 607 Squadron, along with other AAF squadrons, was born in adversity and was made up of 'part-time' fliers. With the end of the Second World War, the AAF Squadrons were quickly disposed of, before being reborn once more, this time as Royal Auxiliary Air Force. As with the original squadron, there were those who saw the squadron of the RAAF as being separate from the squadron of the RAF; it was to be manned by 'part-timers', men willing to give up their spare time to serve their squadron.

The old squadron base of RAF Usworth was to lose 607 Squadron when the unit moved to take up residence at RAF Ouston, Northumberland. Among those that swelled the ranks were members of the original 607 Squadron who had been picked by Leslie Runciman. These men were to remain with the squadron, flying its Spitfires until the radical change to the age of the jet. The old airfield of Usworth was given over to a Japanese car company who built a plant. The North East Aviation Museum, which had also taken up residence on the old airfield, was moved to a distant corner of the land, from where they keep the aviation flag flying.

Those who make the journey to Usworth in search of any remains of 607 Squadron will be more than a bit disappointed. Today, there is virtually nothing left of the squadron, the museum holding little in the way of commemoration of 607 Squadron. A wooden plaque bearing the names of those squadron members who were decorated during the war is about all that remains. The 607 Squadron Association still holds its annual reunion in Durham City, although this is for former members only and serves no purpose to the general public. Hawker Hurricane P2617, a Hurricane that saw service with the squadron in both France and the Battle of Britain, was singled out by Dudley Craig as a possible memorial for a North East Museum. The Hurricane stood on Palace Green in Durham City during a ceremony to mark the disbandment of 607 Squadron, and now resides in the Battle of Britain Hall of the RAF Museum at Hendon. Recent years have also seen the demolition of the old Lamella hangar, built in early 1933 and for so long a feature of Usworth, seen often as a background in the photographs of the day. With its demise another piece of 607 Squadron's history is removed. The last of the squadron's 'originals', Will Whitty, died on 17 November 2003, so bringing to a conclusion the original 607 Squadron. All that is now left is the documentation that marks the passing of 607 Squadron. Memories still surface courtesy of the local press, yet with each passing year 607 Squadron moves further into the distant, murky past. History is another place and another age – presumably 607 Squadron still proudly flies there in a distant shade of blue.

A NOTE ON PILOTS' LOGBOOKS

A logbook, officially known as RAF Form 414, was to be kept by all aircrew. That is to say, every air gunner, navigator, flight engineer and, of course, pilot. Earlier logbooks, issued before the outbreak of the Second World War, tended to be smaller than the later versions issued. The logbooks were hard backed with their backing boards cloth bound. The official title, Form 414, was carried on the front with the owner's name signed in ink in various styles. The object of the logbook was to log every flight carried out by its owner, no matter what the duration of that flight was. Sometimes this was mere minutes, but it had to be logged in the official document. Endorsements, whether good or bad, were also placed in this book. Periodically, this was checked by a senior officer, usually the flight commander, who stamped and signed it.

So, what could be found in a logbook? Well, the basics were a requirement. This consisted of the date of the flight; some even including the exact time of take-off. The type of aircraft that was flown was also entered, as well as its individual number. However, there were to be small differences. For some, the number meant just that and that was all that was included. For others, the interpretation of number meant aircraft individual code letter, such as aircraft 'B', while others would add both in variations. This could be number first, at the top with the letter following down the page until a new aircraft was entered. Some noted both number and aircraft letter.

If the pilot were flying a single-seat aircraft, he would enter 'self' in the column for first pilot. If he were flying as a passenger, he would enter the pilot's name and would enter 'self' in the column for second pilot or passenger. The 'duty' is also entered and this can be any movement of the aircraft, whether it is merely travelling between two bases or carrying out aerobatics or a patrol. The duration of the flight is also added, whether it is minutes or hours. The second side of the logbook is for personal comments, normally of the type that describes a combat or the enemy aircraft that were sighted and attacked.

A logbook, in many ways, can reflect the personality and nature of its owner. For some, the word 'basic' was taken literally. The logbook of Jim Bazin moves along these lines. He merely states the date, aircraft type and number. In the duty column he keeps to the basics, such as 'operational' being the description of a flight. This appears at the height of the Battle of Britain and is a little disappointing. However, we have to bear in mind that he, like all other pilots, wrote the document as part of his profession and with no thought for future historians who may come along. He had, of course, done worse in the Battle of France. On some occasions he covers two-week periods only, with the word Gladiator or Hurricane and not even a number in sight. He did, however, have an excuse for this. In his hurried exit from France his logbook was dumped or lost, and so his entries covering this period were entered at a later date from memory or scraps of paper.

For some, however, the logbook was almost a personal diary, verging on a scrapbook. Aircraft numbers as well as aircraft individual code letters are recorded with equal precision. Under 'duty' can be found what is almost a detailed description of the flights recorded. The type of flight, carried out between which locations, at a certain height and in this direction. The second page offered an area to record various comments such as type of enemy aircraft encountered over the name given, again including were heights and directions. Pieces of a personal nature were also added, such as 'P/O [name] killed today'. This area was used for personal photographs, the logbook almost becoming a supplement of the owner's photo album; quite often these photographs appear nowhere else. A good example of this is the logbook of Dudley Craig. In it can be found photographs of other pilots of the squadron and, in some cases, aircraft that do not appear anywhere else, not even in his own photograph albums. Logbooks like this become an even more important documentary source of reference.

A number of pilots who took part in the Battle of France left their logbooks behind in that country. For some, like Wilkinson Barnes, personnel were simply not allowed on the ships evacuating servicemen from France, space being a premium. Personal kit, including his logbook, ended up in Dunkirk Harbour. For others who served in either, or both, the Battle of France and the Battle of Britain, these logbooks are a much sought-after historical source. As has already been stated, so many names and photographs feature in these logbooks, and they are prized historical artefacts.

For many, the war was the end and they failed to come out the other end. The Ministry of Defence stored their logbooks, whether they were killed or posted as 'missing in action', until the 1960s. Adverts then appeared in the national press, asking relatives or next of kin to come forward and claim the logbooks. Many did claim the logbooks; however, many failed to do so. The result was a selected few were retained and are held mainly in the Public Records Office at Kew. A further number were retained by the RAF Museum at Hendon. For the rest, it was a sad tale, as they went up in smoke.

The squadron had its own version of the logbook: this was the Operational Record Book, known as the ORB. This was virtually the squadron diary. Once more, like the logbooks, they vary greatly and were written usually at the whim of the squadron intelligence officer. In the ORB can be found the details of the day-to-day running of the squadron.

We are given all the movements of and within the squadron. The names of all the pilots who arrived and departed are entered. Normally their previous unit is named, and likewise, the unit that they depart to is also named, giving a guide to how the pilot has passed through the various units of the RAF. Like the logbook, the ORB can be seen as a valuable source in tracing a pilot's or squadron's history. Some pilots get a mention in the ORB only when they came or went, and if we rely wholly on the ORB, it gives the impression that they did nothing in between!

When studied alongside the logbook, the ORB can often be seen to be at variance with the former. Dates can be inaccurately noted and names incorrectly spelt. Mainly, however, this can be down to the fact that the ORB, in some cases, may have been written only once a month. For the officer writing it there may have been a lot of looking back as well as searching among various pieces of paper. Much could have been missed during the Battle of France and Battle of Britain periods. As with the pilots' logbooks, many of the ORBs were either dumped or just left behind in France. This certainly was the case of 607 Squadron's ORB. Most of the squadron's paperwork was left behind in France due to the rapid advance of the German forces and the equally rapid departure of the British forces – paperwork was not the most important thing to save during this period. Today, like some of the logbooks, the squadron ORBs are housed in the Public Records Office at Kew.

EXPLANATORY NOTES

Me 109 and Me 110 – Throughout the text I refer to the term Me 109 or Me 110 when referring to the German fighters Messerschmitt 109 or 110, as opposed to the term Bf 109 or Bf 110 more commonly used today. This is solely to keep a continuity with the contemporary texts and records. The majority of contemporary airmen referred to the term 'Me' when referring to the German fighters.

The RAF Fighter Command basic operating unit, in the period covered by the text, was the squadron. A squadron was normally made up of around twelve to fifteen aircraft, depending on serviceability, the normal fighting number being around twelve. Each squadron was divided into two flights, 'A' and 'B' Flight, each flight being led by a Flight Commander and the whole squadron coming under the command of a Squadron Leader. Each flight was further sub-divided into two sections with Red and Yellow Sections forming 'A' Flight and Blue and Green Sections forming 'B' Flight. Each section was led by a more experienced pilot who could, especially during the early part of the war, be of any flying rank.

The basic operating unit of the Luftwaffe was the Geschwader. Jagdgeschwader (fighter wing) and Kampfgeschwader (bomber wing). The whole of the Geschwader came under the command of the Geschwaderkommodore. Each Geschwader was made up of three or four Gruppen, although a fifth Gruppe was sometimes employed. Each Gruppen in turn was formed from three Stafflen, and each Gruppe had a Stab Flight (a Staff Flight). A Staffel was basically similar to the RAF squadron and normally numbered ten to sixteen aircraft, with the Staffel being under the command of a StaffelKapitan.

For fighting purposes, a Staffel was normally formed by three sub-groups of four aircraft – a Schwarm, which was divided into two Rotte (a pair), flown by a leader and his wingman. While the RAF squadrons were normally divided into groups of thre, flying in 'Vic' formation, this formation was a continuation from pre-war training and was to remain well into the Battle of Britain. The Luftwaffe's Schwarms were flown in 'Finger Four' formation. This formation allowed greater flexibility within the formation, leaving each pilot to look around and search the sky rather than concentrating on flying in formation. If attacked, it allowed the formation much more manoeuvrability when they broke formation.

EQUIVALENT RANKS

RAF	*Luftwaffe*
Wing Commander	Oberstleutnant
Squadron Leader	Major
Flight Lieutenant	Hauptmann
Flying Officer	Oberleutnant
Pilot Officer	Leutnant
Warrant Officer	Oberfeldwebel
Flight Sergeant	Feldwebel
Sergeant	Unteroffizier
Corporal	Obergefreiter
Aircraftman First Class	Gerfreiter
Aircraftman Second Class	Flieger

BIBLIOGRAPHY

Addison, P., and Crang, J.A. (eds), *The Burning Blue*. (Pimlico, 2000)

Beedle, J., *43 Squadron Royal Flying Corps Royal Air Force*. (Beaumont Aviation Literature, 1966)

Bingham, V.F., *Blitzed: Battle of France, 1940*. (Air Research, 1990)

Bowyer, C., *Hurricane at War*. (Allen, 1976)

Bungay, S., *The Most Dangerous Enemy: A History of the Battle of Britain*. (Aurum Press, 2001)

Cull, B. Lander, B., and Weiss, H., *Twelve Days In May*. (Grub Street, 1995)

Dixon, R., *A Gathering of Eagles*. (Publish America, 2005)

Franks, N., *The Air Battle of Dunkirk*. (Kimber, 1983)

Hunt, L., *Twenty-One Squadrons: The History of the Royal Auxiliary Air Force 1925–1957*. (Crecy Books, 1992)

Hastings, S., *Rosamond Lehmann: A Life*. (Chatto and Windus, 2002)

Johnson, J.E., *Wing Leader*. (Chatto and Windus, 1956)

Johnstone AVM, S., *Spitfire into War*. (William Kimber, 1986)

Kershaw, I., *Making Friends With Hitler – Lord Londonderry and Britain's Road to War*. (Allen Lane, 2004)

Mason, F.K., *The Hawker Hurricane*. (Macdonald, 1962)

Mason, F.K., *Battle Over Britain*. (Aston Publications, 1990)

Occleshaw, M., *The Romanov Conspiracies – The Romanovs and the House of Windsor*. (Chapman's Publishers, 1993)

Quill, J., *Spitfire: A Test Pilot's Story*. (John Murray, 1983)

Ramsey, W.G. (ed.), *The Battle Of Britain Then And Now Mk V*. (After The Battle, 1989)

Rawlings, J., *Fighter Squadrons of the RAF and their Aircraft*. (Crecy, 1966)

Richey, P., *Fighter Pilot*. (B.T. Batsford, 1941)

Robertson, B. , *Spitfire: The Story of a Famous Fighter*. (Harleyford, 1960)

Robinson, A., *RAF Fighter Squadrons of the Battle of Britain*. (Arms and Armour, 1987)

Rollings, C., *Wire And Walls: RAF Prisoners of War In Itzahoe, Spangenberg And Thorn 1939–1942*. (Ian Allan Publishing, 2003)

Ross, T. (ed.), *75 Eventful Years of the Royal Air Force 1918–1993*. (Wingham Aviation Books, 1993)

Smith, R.C., *Hornchurch Offensive: The Definitive Account of the RAF Fighter Airfield, Its Pilots, Groundcrew and Staff, Vol. 2*. (Grub Street, 2001)

Shacklady, E., *Hawker Hurricane*. (NPI Media Group, 2000)

Shores, C., and Williams, C., *Aces High*. (Neville Spearman, 1986)

Shores, C., *Aces High, Vol. 2*. (Grub Street, 1999)

Shores, C., *Those Other Eagles: A Tribute to the British, Commonwealth and Free European Fighter Pilots who Claimed Between Two and Four Victories in Aerial Combat, 1939–1982*. (Grub Street, 2004)

Sweetman, J., *Tirpitz: Hunting The Beast*. (Naval Institute Press, 2000)

Townsend, P., *Time and Chance*. (Collins, 1978)

Welford, H., *The Unrelenting Years 1916–1946*. (Newton, 1996)

Wood, D., and Dempster, D., *The Narrow Margin*. (Hutchinson, 1961)

Wynn, K.G., *The Men of the Battle of Britain*. (Gliddon Books, 1989)

INDEX

Note: A letter 'N' following a page number indicates that the reference on that page is within an endnote.